Smart Teacher

Teacher Career & Retirement Planning

Nicole van Woudenberg

Table of Contents

Preface   4

Part 1: Stages of Your Career

    1 The Early Years   8

    2 The Middle years   27

    3 The Later, Senior Years   41

    4 The Last Five Years   51

Part 2: Reinvention and Moving On

    5 Pivot or Alternatives   68

    6 Licensing in Other Jurisdictions   75

    7 Reinvention Stories   91

Part 3: Appendices and Endnotes

    8 Appendix 1 Reading List   101

    9 Appendix 2 Basic Needs Budget Template 104

    10 Appendix 3 Personal Goals in Retirement 108

    11 Endnotes   113

About the Author   118

Preface

I was merely six years into my teaching career (just hit 30!) when I attended my first retirement workshop. With trepidation and some confused looks in my direction, I joined the buffet line loading my plate with the free dinner promised prior to the presentation. The place was buzzing, lots of chatter and hearing repeatedly: "How many more years do you have to reach 85?" That's teacher speak for the formula used to reach full-pension benefits in Ontario. Obviously, my youth gave me away and I got a direct: "You're certainly nowhere near retirement age" from a jovial kindergarten teacher ahead of me in the line. I agreed and joked I was there for the free food since I didn't yet get paid enough to cover the basics. "It's good that you're starting early. I wish I had started at your age as my pension is my biggest asset." She asked me to join her table where I met her colleagues.

All were within their last five years of teaching and this being their first retirement workshop. "So what motivated you to come to this when you're just starting in your career?" one of the teachers asked. I explained that with all the deductions from my paycheque, and pension contributions being one of the biggest, I figured it was important for me to learn more about it.

The presentation started as we were finishing the last of the sweet desserts.   I don't remember exactly what I learned in my first of several retirement workshops I attended throughout my career – but I did win a door prize that really got the crowd riled up as I was nowhere near retirement and should not be rewarded with a union branded bag savoured by those who had already put in at least twenty years!   Teachers love free stuff and are quite savvy when it comes to collecting items for their students and classes. However, what I learned that day is that most teachers are so passionate about their students and teaching that they wait too long to shape and foster their passions for a fruitful and rewarding second chapter called retirement.

The purpose of this book is to support Canadian teachers plan their career and eventual retirement: no matter what province you live in; no matter if this is your - first and only - or second career and; no matter if you're an early, middle or late career teacher. This book will provide you with the framework to enjoy the present and feel secure about the future. You can start anywhere in the book, depending on your career stage. However, don't neglect the early years if you are a middle- or later-career teacher because you may still be able to implement some of the useful suggestions. It is important to talk about and share ideas with others.   You may have more in common with someone who has been teaching as long as you have but learn from those younger and older. The book includes real-life reinvention stories: some teachers leaving before full-pension and others sticking it out to retirement age or beyond. Discover how they are living their best life and many using their skillset to delve into different passion projects. You can also join our online community on Facebook,

Instagram as well as follow the *85 After School* podcast. Teachers – whether retired or not – love to share their knowledge and teach others so this is your community to tap into for suggestions, strategies and advice. Meet you there!

Part 1

Stages of Your Career

CHAPTER ONE

The Early years

The first five years of teaching are all about survival, navigating the system and establishing yourself within your school and the larger community. It is also a time of brutal honesty, especially if this is your first career and you are in your twenties. If you don't enjoy working with students, or the specific age group: change. Do not stay. You're doing yourself a favour, your colleagues and, most importantly, the children. When you're brutally honest and say teaching isn't what I thought it would be and I do not enjoy it, you know it's time to make a change. You have many transferable skills and can pivot into other, and probably, more lucrative careers (see Chapter 5). Those who are coming to the profession as a second-career choice have reflected and explored the profession. It is assumed that if teaching is your second career you have made a conscious decision of returning to school to gain your credentials (in some provinces a sixteen-month program) and are less likely to leave the profession once securing a full-time position. Hence, if in your first-five years you are only staying for the pension: don't. I know some will completely disagree with me, but considering that your working life is long, anywhere between 30 and 35 years, wouldn't you rather be doing something that you enjoy most of the time rather than hating it nearly every single day? So be wise. Use your first five years to establish yourself, secure a full-time position and determine if this truly is the right career choice or are you just sticking around for the pension, vacation days and benefits?

Now that we got that out of the way, let's focus on the ten strategies that you can implement during the first five years of teaching to make the most of your career.

Strategy 1:

Secure a Full-Time Position as Soon as Possible.

Depending on the supply and demand for certified teachers, there may be a period of time where full-time positions are very competitive. Even though some provinces gather statistical information[1] in relation to employability of newly certified teachers, there still seems to be a pattern of extreme needs in a twenty-year cycle followed by the next five to ten years of overabundance. The political climate between teachers' unions and the ruling government plays a factor in whether applicants to Faculties of Education see the profession as desirable. Nevertheless, for many teachers, it's a calling, a passion, a vocation and we pursue teaching for those reasons.

When I say secure a full-time position, be sure to secure it in a school district's geographical area where you wish to live. There have been many teachers who secured a full-time position only to realize later that in a time of teacher abundance, you cannot get full-time work in another district (unless, perhaps you speak French) and even if you do, your seniority may not carry over to the other district even if it is the same union. So do your homework. Apply to all the districts and chartered schools in which you're eligible to teach (e.g. Public, Catholic, French etc.) if they participate in the teachers' pension.

If you don't secure full-time work, put in your time to substitute (supply) teach. Be eager. Do not turn down substitute jobs even if you never saw yourself as a Kindergarten teacher. This is your opportunity (even for a half-day) to determine if your gut feeling was right or if you can see yourself in that position. Remember also in some provinces there is a big difference whether you start in elementary, middle or high school. Again, you may not be qualified to get a full-time job in a panel in which you're not certified to teach but you can get your feet wet. Discover by substitute teaching if it is something you want to pursue even if you weren't qualified from University studies. Once in-service (i.e. graduated and certified) you can find avenues to become certified to teach in the panel you thought previously not available to you. But I'm getting ahead of myself. Part-time work allows you to network and make connections. It gets your name out there even if there is a seniority system of hiring. Collective bargaining agreements (CBA), the contracts between the school board (employer) and the union (employee group), clearly outline what the process is for occasional teachers being hired to full-time positions. Familiarize yourself with the process fully and if you have questions, ask your union representative.

Strategy 2:

Read Your CBA & Benefits; Know Your CBA and Benefits!

Whether you're a permanent contract teacher or occasional teacher, get a copy of all the CBAs in your School Board (but mainly yours). For those in non-unionized environments, be sure to understand your contract before you sign. Read specifically about surplus[2], recalls and redundancies: this is in the event of over-supply of employees when enrolment numbers for the following school year are predicted to be less. Early career-teachers are often affected by fluctuations of enrolment in their first five years. Also, read about managerial rights to move you to another school. For example, the Board has a job for you, but it could be more than 50 km away from where you live. This is why it is important you know your rights. This will allow you to push your union representatives to file grievances should management not have followed the expectations of your working conditions such as transfers, travel allowances between schools, or preparation time. Always be aware of your seniority status. Often lists are created for a school and a district. You have the right to ask about your seniority status as well as access your personnel file at the district office should it ever be necessary. All of this should be described in your CBA. This is why it is so important that you familiarize yourself with it early in your career. Most teachers take the word of others or repeat things that they've heard that may not even be true. My favourite that I have heard repetitively is that one teacher is going to "grieve" another teacher. That is not possible. The CBA is between the union group and the employer. If you have a complaint about another teacher, there are professional steps that are more appropriately outlined in School Board policies and procedures, or a provincial regulator, not the CBA. So get yourself a copy and read the sections most relevant to you in the first five years: pay scale, additional responsibility pay scale, sick-leave benefits, maternity/ parental leave, transfers, mileage paid (if you travel to workshops or between schools), benefits (if embedded in your CBA), teacher evaluations – to name but a few.

Medical and other benefits offered may not be clearly outlined in any document. Often those beginning their careers are unaware of what they are entitled to until they require a service. I would recommend that you check your coverage as soon as you have access. Call the provider or set-up your online account given your plan number. Ask about single and family coverage. Find out what your coverage is for dental, eyesight, naturopath, psychology/ therapist, physiotherapy and massage allowances. Use what you need. Your employer may also offer you automatic life insurance (minimal amount). Be sure if there is a need to designate a beneficiary that you do that as well. This is part of your compensation and you are entitled to it when needed. The nuances are in the details so be sure to check specifically how much you have left in any cycle. For example, if you require eyeglasses, you may only purchase them every twenty-four months (not necessarily two calendar years). Scaling (or teeth cleaning) may be every nine months not twice a year. Look for providers who offer to directly bill your insurance company. This will save you the hassle of submitting a claim. If you require medication and specifically need the brand name (not the generic) due to possible side effects, be sure to have your doctor's prescription specify it. These are all cost-effective ways to minimize your out-of-pocket costs when your job provides you with these benefits. Benefits will change throughout your career so be sure to stay on top of it and if you do pay upfront, submit your claims immediately after the service otherwise you're leaving money on the table. One last point, your employer may also offer Employee Assistance Program (EAP) as part of your benefits that are offered by a different provider than your medical and dental plan. The EAP may offer a range of services from free legal advice to grief counselling. Usually information about this services is posted in your workplace.

Strategy 3:

Join Your Association and Professional Organizations

You pay union dues. Make that work for you. Get involved. Go to the general annual meetings. Become the representative at your school. Find out about professional development funds available to you through your local and provincial union. Often there are grants awarded to members for taking courses, attending conferences or even full-year scholarships. Research the members-only section of your local and provincial union to determine what is available. It may also be in your union bylaws at both levels. You can always just directly ask your representatives. If they don't know, keep asking. Consider running for an executive position. Many of the unions now have a spot available for beginning career teachers. Often positions at the local level go uncontested meaning you don't even have to have a major campaign, just get your friends to vote for you.

There are many benefits to being active in your association. Besides the opportunities for learning and increasing your labour knowledge, your involvement may open up doors to other opportunities. For example, through my union, I was sponsored as a participant in Project Overseas, a volunteer program to co-facilitate workshops for teachers in other countries during the summer months (organized by the Canadian Teachers Federation). I was also selected to go through the leadership program, serve as committee chair, receive both learning funds and some pretty nice union branded clothing that I still wear!

Find out if your employer is a member of specific professional organizations that provide you access to member-only sections of websites or resources. Start with your subject association or talk to colleagues who are part of a professional association and find out how they became involved. Many have minimal membership fees, but see if you can get free access by affiliation first. Some of the best-known professional organizations (ISTE, ASCD, CCEC) need volunteers during their conferences, which will either provide you with a discount to attend or allow you to attend for free.

If there are no professional organizations that are of interest to you, what aspect of the teaching profession does interest you? Are you interested in music or the arts? Consider starting a group of your own with colleagues who have similar interests. Often there are grant applications available through your union or the government. Reach out to your employer's program support staff, such as a curriculum consultant or regional superintendent to ask if such grants exist or if they can connect you to anyone in the district who has been awarded such grants in the past. Learn from those who have received funding in the past.

Strategy 4:

Micro-credentials

Use your summer months to re-energize. Also use it to build your resumé further. Research if you will be paid more if you have extra qualifications. Some jurisdictions require on-going education. This may be as simple as reading professional journals or participating in a workshop. Much of the in-service provided to beginning teachers is either through a formal or informal mentoring program. Be sure to articulate the skills you gain on your resumé. There is increased demand for teachers who understand and teach students with special education needs or English language learners. Canada is a country of immigrants, even if you are working in a rural area, you will encounter students with differing learning needs. See if you can access free courses or receive funding to take courses that will enhance your resumé and potentially increase your pay by moving on the pay grid. In Ontario for example, you not only move through an annual grid with an increase in pay but you also can move latterly depending on the courses you've taken (called QECO). In Quebec, you may be paid for running a club after school based on a specific skill or certification you have. For example, running a cooking club because you have restaurant experience, may qualify for the paid extra-curricular activity. One of my favourite clubs that an educator was paid to run was the "nail club". At the one-hour after-school meeting, participants worked on artfully painting fingernails.

Find out what you need to do in order to get to the higher paid salaries in the education system. If you're aiming for a possible management job (principal, superintendent, director, leader in an educational organization such as provincial union or government) consider completing a Masters degree. And remember, there may be funding available for you to take the courses that lead to your Masters degree. But be wise: research what is required and decide if you want to box yourself in with an M.Ed. or be more open-ended with an M.A. in a subject not necessarily directly tied to Education if you ever want to pivot from the education sector. For example, if you study political science, you can move on to working for a political party or a think tank. Micro-credentials are most important for the knowledge you'll gain which support your students' learning but they also provide you with an advantage over other colleagues who do not have your skillset. Furthermore, many employers provide you with a pay bump once you have another degree. You may not recuperate the money spent on tuition with that pay bump but it does open up positions where the pay will be higher. Weigh the pros and cons before leaping into further study. Know exactly what you hope to gain from it.

Last, you may also wish to explore the steps to be credentialed in another province. At the time of writing, Canada has professional transferability that permits teachers who are certified to teach in one province to be certified in another province. The reason to explore this in your first five years is because your degree is newly minted. If things change in the future, and you're twenty years in, the laws of mobility may have changed. Read more about licensing in other jurisdiction in Chapter 6 to determine if this is something you wish to pursue. I am personally licensed in five jurisdictions including three provinces and two European countries. It wasn't a lot of effort to go through the process, it just requires patience, so this is something you can undertake as well.

Strategy 5:

Get to the Top of the Pay Grid ASAP

The previous strategy may assist you to reach the top of the pay grid quickly. Does your previous work experience count towards your grid placement when you're first hired? Never hurts to ask if your three months of supply teaching with another employer helps bump you up on the years of experience list. Most unionized environments have very specific rules about how to get to the top of the grid but your overseas teaching experience or work in a private school prior to you being licensed may count.

If there is ability to move on the grid for both experience and qualifications, be sure to find out what exactly you need in order to move both horizontally and vertically. For example, in Ontario, QECO determines your status in a Category (horizontal) based on the education you have achieved. At any time, you can move yourself to a higher category by taking the appropriate course. Be sure to check that your course qualifies so that it will benefit you on the pay grid.

Strategy 6:

Sign Up for Pension News

You're probably thinking this is extremely premature but the more you know about the structure of your pension the better you can take care of what will be one of the (if not "the") biggest assets you will own. Once you are vested (usually after one year full-time but this varies), you are able to set up an account and monitor your contributions. Look at your paycheque. You'd be surprised how often mistakes are made. Are the deductions correct? Is the percentage of union dues and your pension correct for the salary you are making? Compare your contributions to the amount listed in your pension account. It would be wise for you to review your statements on a yearly basis. Put a reminder in your calendar around mid-October to go online (paperless statements are now the norm). When you login to your member's account, check that you've been credited for your full-time year of service, the amount you have contributed is accurate and explore what is predicted to be your pension should you stay full-time at your current salary. Observe if there are any changes to your contribution rate. If this isn't clear on the statement, check your pay-stub or contact the plan's administrator directly. Remember they are there because of you, so you are entitled to their service.

You would be wise to also look at the commuted value, if it is listed on your annual statement. Commuted value is a lump sum of money, which is a pay-out in lieu of the monthly pension payments. It is important for you to know your commuted value should you leave your current province, change careers, or other life choices where you wish to take your savings with you. Note that there are lots of rules surrounding taking your money out of the pension and you'd be wise to know at a high-level what that encompasses. For example, commuted value fluctuates as it is based on actuary tables and looks at your profile (age, years of service, salary, contributions-to-date etc.) for such calculations. Your statement may provide the following explanation:

> "The commuted value depends on several factors including your age, amount of your pension, your qualifying years and bond yields. It also fluctuates considerably when bond yields

or the calculation basis changes. The commuted value of your pension can be transferred to a locked-in retirement account, to another registered pension plan or to a life income fund. The money must be locked in and can only be used to provide you with a lifetime retirement income. (The Income Tax Act does however restrict the amount that can be transferred tax-free)... It is designed to give you an idea of the benefit payable if you leave the plan before retirement."[3]

For purposes of understanding commuted value, ten years into my career with a salary of around $70,000 I had contributed roughly $51,000 (including interest) and my commuted value was estimated at $126,000. At the fifteen-year mark with a salary of close to $100 thousand and $117 thousand contributed, the commuted value was estimated at $324 thousands. Again, the commuted value is all based on the calculation factors and you would be wise to find out in your annual statement what the estimate is for you personally. I recognize that some pension statements no longer include the commuted value, so you may have to contact your pension plan administrators directly to find out. It is not that you wish to take out your money but it is to get an understanding of the 'replacement' value of your pension should you exit before monthly retirement payments begin (as early as 50 years of age).

Next, learn who else makes contributions to your pension. This is typically a dual-relationship: the government (employer) and you make contributions. Many in the general public forget the part where teachers are contributing up to 14% of their salary to their pension. It is a good pension as it is defined (meaning you receive a set monthly amount, usually adjusted for inflation). In 2021, less than 25% of

Canadians still had a defined pension plan[4] and even though there have been changes made over the years and threats to this changing even for government employees, it looks like it will remain. There are no guarantees, however, and you should be in the know about who makes decisions about changes to your pension structure.

For example, in Ontario, the plan sponsors are the government and the Ontario Teachers' Federation. Decisions are made through the governing board and the government cannot make unilateral decisions to change benefits or contribution rates[5]. If you are an Ontario teacher I would recommend you read more about the structure of the pension to get a better understanding of its security[6]. In Quebec, teachers contribute to a pension plan for government employees, mainly in the health, social services, education and public service sectors[7]. If you are a teacher in Alberta, you would be wise to read the informative website and watch the beginning teacher videos explaining the plans[8]. The key here is to keep abreast, at a high level, of any changes or news that would impact one of the biggest assets you'll own in your lifetime should you stay for a thirty-year career.

Strategy 7:

Build Your Network

It is so easy to amass a network of teacher friends beyond your school. Look for professional social-media apps that will allow you to connect and learn from other educational professionals, not just teachers. There are many who try to build a brand online as they are either wanting to pivot from classroom teaching or are thinking of post-teaching career opportunities for which a network is a necessity. Beyond the online communities and professional association chat groups in which you can be a participant or an observer, also nurture your face-to-face networks. Go beyond your school and district. Maybe there are regional workshops (paid for by your union funds or school board) that you can attend. Any time there is a callout for beginning teachers to participate in a learning opportunity, apply. You may not be chosen but putting your name out there builds recognition. Having a network allows for further growth and development as you exchange ideas and become recognized for your contributions.

Ask lots of questions, especially if you're interested in pursuing a similar endeavour of someone in your network. Teachers love to share and are generally supportive of one another's endeavours. I remember in my fourth year of teaching, a colleague, who had been teaching for at least ten years, was facilitating three-day summer workshops through our association. I had no idea these courses even existed, let alone that classroom teachers were eligible to lead them. I asked so many questions that she said I should join her and see if I would enjoy co-facilitating parts of the classroom management activities. The following summer, because I knew I had to apply for these instructor opportunities in late winter, I was able to facilitate my own workshop in two different locations. That allowed me to connect with more teachers outside of my school and district and build my network further. All these years later, I'm still in touch with some participants from those workshops!

Strategy 8:

Pay Off Debts and Start Saving

Ugh! Debt. It sucks. We work so hard, way more than the general public even realizes, and in the early years it seems like there's nothing left from our paycheque to even consider saving. Any financial guru who is "worth their salt" will tell you: it is not an income problem; it is an expenditure problem. Although I agree with that mostly, the cost of living, especially in major urban centres, makes it very difficult for beginning teachers who make on average a starting salary of $ 56,000[9]. However, living below your means will get you ahead and once you're ahead, you're sailing, as your salary will only go up. Pay off debt from the highest interest first: credit card, line-of-credit, student loans, car loan, mortgage.

A recent research project by Ramsey Solutions[10] with ten thousand respondents showed that most millionaires did not have high-salary jobs. Teachers ranked in the top three careers (behind engineers and accountants) that are "most likely to have millionaires in their ranks"[10]. Some key take-aways from the study was that teachers started early and stayed consistent in saving and investing. It is hypothesized because teachers work within a system where we do not have the ability to make up our own rules, it shapes us to take the slow and steady approach with discipline. You too can adopt the slow and steady approach and end up as a millionaire one day (and that may be on top of your full pension).

Try to save ten per cent of your gross (before taxes) salary by paying yourself first every paycheque. If you schedule an automatic payment of $100-$200 to your savings account every paycheque, you won't be seeing it in your chequeing account for spending. Slowly but surely you'll accumulate a little nest egg. Some of you may be gasping, saying: "$100! Ya, right, I don't have that to spare". I challenge you to track your spending (every penny) for a week and find out how much you spend on unnecessary lattes, clothing or stuff for your classroom. There are plenty of great books that will help you become a person who lives below their means, just use the library to find them (don't buy them!).

Strategy 9:

Read About Investing

I mentioned the library in the previous strategy. If you have not yet become familiar with all the resources available to you through your public library – stop reading – and immediately go get your free membership (if you're a homeowner, your taxes pay for that service, so go milk it). I see you rolling your eyes, but you have no idea the treasure trove you have at your disposal with your library card: movies, streaming, books, eBooks, magazines, audiobooks, in-person or online courses... and the list goes on. "But there's a waiting list for the book I want" you say. Well either read about the benefits of delayed gratification (the marshmallow experiment, anyone?) or use that gift card that you got in December or June from your mini-fans. Nothing is that pressing that you can't wait for the item. Besides, many libraries order more copies when they see the waiting list grow. I've never had to wait the reported 30 weeks for an item when I first put it on hold, I'd say 8 weeks at most.

I should have made Join The Library it's own section so you could've skipped my soapbox rant above, however, the reason I'm so passionate about the library's wealth of resources has to do with investing. You need to learn the basics about investing. I know you know you have a good pension – defined benefit (DBPP) – and you don't think you need to really do anything else for retirement saving. You're wrong! It is very important that you learn the basics so you can build wealth alongside your guaranteed income from your DBPP. Do you know what most employers are offering their employees, if they even offer any retirement benefits? It is called defined-contribution (DCPP). Once you learn more about it, you'll realize that your DBPP is the golden nest egg everyone admires but is rarely available anymore. Learn about stocks, bonds, REITs and the various ways you can invest. Determine your personality and how much risk you're willing to take on. The major banks usually have a 'practice' investment account. You can pretend to buy stocks with fake money and see how a portfolio does over the course of a year without risking any real money. If you can't easily find the practice investment portfolio, call your bank and ask them how to find it in your online account.

Start with resources (books) that focus on Canadian terms and that are knowledge-accessible to you. If you pick up a book that is too advanced you'll lose interest and not commit to learning how to grow your wealth. A list of introductory books that helped me is listed in Appendix 1.

Strategy 10:

Don't Buy School / Work Stuff with Your Own Money

This is a no-brainer yet so many teachers feel the need to purchase items for their classroom. You're a professional, you earn money for your teaching skills. You shouldn't have to use your own money to buy things to do your job! Seriously, name me a dentist or lawyer that you know who uses their personal money to buy legal pads, pens, or dental instruments to do their job. And they are professionals like you! So there you have it, stop buying school supplies or things you need to do your job with your own money. I learned the hard way when I started tracking my money in the first couple of years of my career. One year it was almost $1,500! And I'm probably on the lower end of teachers who spend money on items that should be supplied to you as an employee. In the end it's your choice: you can buy things for your classroom because you believe you need them to do your job or invest that money instead. If I had invested that $1,500 twenty-five years ago, instead of buying things for my classroom (things that I no longer own by the way), I'd have at least $4,000 today[11]. I'm not being selfish, I'm being practical and realistic.

Think of alternative ways to get items for free. Check websites like Freecycle, Kijiji, Craig's List, FB Marketplace to name but a few. There are several websites like *donorschoose* that fulfill teachers' classroom wishes. Again, ask your school administrator for the items required. Maybe in the monthly newsletter or website, you're allowed to petition the community for items needed. In one of my schools, the students in their woodworking class would make the bookshelves some teachers desperately needed for their textbooks. If there is a budget crunch, and your principal can't provide funding, ask them, or the district head, if there are outside funds that you are allowed to access or if you can apply for grants. The squeaky wheel gets the oil so don't be discouraged by the first "no". Heck with a "no" you're further ahead than by not asking at all.

Beginning Years Summed Up

There you have the ten strategies that will help you jump-start your teaching career into a successful one. Reread the strategies that resonated with you and explore the footnotes and suggested materials in Appendix 1. Not all strategies will be applicable given your personal situation but they will make you think about what works in your current position. The key here is to think, engage, discuss and explore these ideas with others as well. Join our community online and engage with those who are in the same position as you or those who have been there.

CHAPTER TWO

The Middle Years

Congratulations! You are well settled into your career as a teacher. You truly enjoy working with students, even when some days are challenging. You have learned exponentially about your own skills and where you excel in your teaching. Perhaps you've moved to different schools or crossed panels. It is fair to say you have found your groove and you now have a predictable income and security. You're comfortable, or getting there. There may have been some major life changes for you along the way: a partnership, house purchase, and the birth of your child. For those who entered teaching as a second career you may have had to navigate changes as well: teenagers at home, perhaps a divorce, a move to another home, aging-parent responsibilities. However, through all this, you have managed to balance work and personal life better than in your beginning-years where you probably took work home at night and perhaps even went into school on the weekends. You've reached your middle years and now it is time to work smarter not harder.

The strategies in Chapter 1 still apply in this stage of your career. The next ten to fifteen years are to explore and maximize your skills, income and position within your school and district. But you are also building skills that will be transferable beyond this environment. Let's discuss three foci for the middle years that will help you excel.

Focus 1:

Educational Lifer

You love what you do and you are indeed a lifelong learner. Every challenge is a way for you to explore solutions and solve problems. This is what feeds your soul and you thrive on the daily "ah-ha" moments from you and your students. If this describes you, you are probably aiming to learn as much throughout your career as you did in the beginning years. The middle years provide you with the opportunity to vary your experiences. Don't fear grade or subject changes, embrace them, learn from them. Seek out other levels of responsibility: department head, chair of your subject, lead-teacher, or mentor a beginning teacher. All these opportunities allow you to learn more about your style of leadership, build your resumé, as well as possibly receive additional pay or allowances. If you think you want to become a principal, sign-up to be the teacher-in-charge or fill-in for the absence of your school administrator. Most of the time this role also comes with designated pay (check your CBA).

You will want to explore what other opportunities exist to compliment your development as a leader. I know when I completed my Masters, and because I held special education qualifications, I was able to teach an additional qualification course for not only my association but a University as well. Most of these courses have moved to online learning formats and as long as you are organized, you are able to easily manage your full-time work with the expectations of teaching such a course. You may also be asked to be a guest presenter for which an honorarium may be provided. Teaching adults, your peers, is a great way to develop leadership skills for you to eventually move toward a managerial position at a school. The extra salary earned by facilitating courses or workshops is an added bonus.

In a similar way, there is always a callout for classroom teachers to host a student-teacher. This is a great way to practise your leadership skills. Developing skills to provide constructive feedback will serve you well when you have to complete evaluations of your staff once you're a principal. Moreover, being an associate teacher rewards you with a stipend or honorarium. Although it may not seem like a lot, change your perspective and consider that you're being paid to develop your leadership skills which will pay off when you are putting your candidacy portfolio together to move to administration. And you don't necessarily have to have many years of teaching experience. If you are an innovative teacher who excels in developing engaging curriculum, the number of years you've been teaching will be a secondary consideration.

If being a school administrator isn't for you, find out if there are other roles of responsibility like a consultant, coach or master-teacher that would allow you to be exposed to a community of schools and a larger group of teachers whom you'd support. You would then have expanded your teaching skills to include adults. Find out from individuals currently in the role what the job entails on a daily basis.

Ask them what they like about it and what are some of the challenges they encounter.

As recommended for beginning teachers, join an association on your employer's dime. They may require volunteer presenters at their next conference. Offer to present in your field of expertise or look for summer job or training opportunities. Start a YouTube channel that teaches others strategies to use in their classroom. Similar to me teaching courses for teachers, apply to local college or continuing education departments to teach your expertise. One of my colleagues loved travel and spoke Spanish fluently. Although she did not teach Spanish at her school, she pitched a course to not only her local college but the public library as well and taught Spanish for Travellers which was very popular.

Create something unique in your classroom that gets the attention of your administrator and district staff. A colleague of mine in another district created a unique partnership between her kindergartners and the nearby retirement home. The intergenerational project got the attention of district staff and she was featured on the news for the positive impact it had on both the children and the elderly residents (they were much gentler with one another after visiting their pseudo grandparents). Self-promoting your curriculum or ideas that show metrics of student growth in learning is a must. Don't be shy or think you are boasting. A good idea needs to be shared. Marketing does not come naturally to most teachers but it is a skill that we should learn to a greater degree.

If indeed you find that you are striving to climb the educational ladder, be sure to get your leadership credentials. Strategy 4 in the first chapter provides suggestions. Managing adults is a lot different than managing students. Learn about your leadership-style[12], your emotional intelligence and work on improving in the areas where you may struggle.

Focus 2:

Pivot or Post-Career Passions

Some of you love the classroom, hate work-politics and do not want to manage or lead other teachers. You don't see yourself becoming a principal, superintendent or head of a district. No problem. You are in the perfect position to hone your skills in the passion of your choice. What do you thoroughly enjoy? What gets your juices flowing? What topics or activities get you excited? Usually it is something we try to incorporate into our teaching.

A younger teacher I was mentoring loved arts and crafts. She would take any opportunity in the curriculum to integrate an art activity to have her students demonstrate their learning. When she went off on maternity leave with twins, she missed being able to have students create works of art. She channelled that creativity into sewing costumes for her twins. Her tutu was a hit and considering her network of teachers, who were also having babies, she started to sell her tutus. Soon she had a semi-online order process and she couldn't sew fast enough to fill the orders. She made a nice little profit on each of the tutus. After her maternity leave, she tried to keep it going but with full-time work and motherhood, it wasn't a 'fun' thing to do anymore so the business closed.

Another colleague loved baking and cake decorating. She excelled in the process of creating personalized cakes for colleagues. Through word of mouth, she would get at least two or three orders a month. She enjoyed the creative outlet and made a little profit on each cake. Likewise, the teacher who replaced me when I moved into a specialized position, had years of construction experience. His summers were spent building decks or completing basements. He loved the work and the extra money allowed for reinvesting into a second property he now owns.

Starting a side hustle may not be as easy as it sounds. First, if you're not sure what side hustle you should start, you probably need more time to find something you're passionate about or that you're already doing for free to help others. But before you start putting your own money into this endeavour, do some research and calculate your cost (materials and time). The summer months allow for plenty of uninterrupted time to plan and prepare or execute your side hustle. Most importantly you need to test it with acquaintances to see if your idea will be sustainable (acquaintances, not friends or family members because they most likely love you and tell you amazing things about your side hustle but won't be repeat customers). Like the tutu and cakes, everything has an expiration date unless you can reinvent and reach a wider audience.

Teaching is a specialized profession and contrary to popular belief not everyone can do it. The skills you possess in order to plan, organize and teach a group of students is not innate. You hone your skills through experience and the continuous professional development offered. Think about your technical and soft skills. You will easily discover that your current skills are transferable to working as, for example, a human resource specialist, technology expert, instructional designer, professional organizer, writer, videographer, photographer or police officer. I'm simplifying but that's exactly what several of my colleagues did mid-career: they pivoted! One became a police officer, another a professional basketball coach, a third started her own yoga studio and yet another started his own winemaking business. Read more about pivoting and part-time work in Chapter 5. The opportunities are endless as long as you do your homework.

Although these individuals decided to leave the teaching profession mid-career, and found success in a second career, if you enjoy teaching, you have plenty of time to pursue these ambitions as a post-teaching career. My personal passion has always been writing. I started in earnest in the summer of Grade 10 when I took a summer course. I have been writing for enjoyment ever since, entertaining my family and friends. With this book, I am expanding to a wider audience. Your experience and the skills you have to fulfil your passion can provide you with an opportunity to pivot or prepare for post-career work.

How do you get there while you're still in your full-time teaching job? Great question. I already shared ideas in chapter one (Strategy 3) that can be applied here. However, let me expand on the ideas in relation to supporting your passion bucket that will provide a fulfilling retirement. As a mid-career teacher you have hopefully expanded your network beyond teachers and those of your generation (if not, get going!). Your current job requires you to teach a curriculum. Your skills allow you to be creative in how you deliver that curriculum. There are funds, grants and outside agencies who set aside money for various creative projects. You need to learn how to write proposals in order to apply for such grants, but what a great way to involve your students and meet curriculum expectations. Say your passion is photography and this is something you really like to pursue in your free time and eventually in retirement. Your creative thinking allows you to connect curriculum expectations and the use of photography to create meaningful learning projects for your students. Should you require equipment or materials that are not available at the school or district, you could seek out funding or write proposals that support your unique project.

Sometimes the school or parent council may even partially support such projects. I have already mentioned websites that provide funding for classroom requests by anonymous donors (e.g. donorschoose.org). We always teach from our strengths and if photography is your passion, your students will see it in the way you use it as a tool to facilitate their learning. You are also more likely to introduce something to students that they may never have been exposed to outside of school. It's a win-win-win situation all around. Not sure how to write proposals? Ask colleagues, find out who has been successful in applying and receiving grants or funds from various organizations and ask them for help. In the end, all these experiences help you further refine what you're good at, what you enjoy and, what passions fill your bucket post-teaching.

There are two important strategies mentioned in the previous chapter that you should consider if indeed you wish to build a side hustle with substance (as opposed to having a hobby you do for enjoyment, not monetary gain). First, teachers in general are not great self-promotors. If you really want to get a side hustle off the ground you should learn marketing strategies that help build and promote your brand. If you don't have any idea of how to brand yourself, start there. There are plenty of free resources on the internet where you can learn how to shape your brand. Second, build a network of your target audience. The next chapter delves into the importance of networking further. Once you have a network, you can expand it by offering free resources that will expand those interested in your brand. You can easily produce such 'freebies' using AI generators. You're skilled at communicating and AI just requires very precise instructions and details in order to generate what you want to create. That's the work smarter, not harder technique. Don't discount the importances of these two strategies.

Focus 3:

Building Your Wealth

The ten- or fifteen-year period in the middle of your career is the time to build your wealth. Now I know many of you have children, who are expensive creatures, but you can still build your wealth by sticking to what I described in Strategy 8, chapter one, as living below your means. Depending on your status (partnered/married, single/ divorced) it would be wise to try and save 15%[13] of your net (after tax) income at this stage. This may be to save for your children's education; it could be for an extra payment to reduce your mortgage or to add to your investment savings. The idea is not to spend it on tangibles like vacations, material possessions (excluding car or home) or anything that adds to your liabilities instead of your assets. Read about building your wealth in the books listed in Appendix 1.

Besides living below your means, you can also try to increase your salary. Maximize your pay as soon as possible with your employer. If mobility and seniority is transferable consider movement to another employer if the pay is much better. But do the math, as it may not be worth it for an increase of a few thousand dollars.

Explore if it is worth it for you to see a "fee-for" financial advisor to develop a wealth plan for you. They may provide insight and advice for investment, build passive income and allow your nest egg to grow parallel to your pension.

I would highly recommend that at the ten-year mark you attend a retirement workshop, usually offered for free by your association or the actual pension plan associates. They will provide you with a high level overview of what you can expect monetarily and how you can explore more using the tools and resources available to you through either the pension plan's members' account (i.e. calculator tools for scenarios) or your association. They will also address insurance and benefits (which typically end when you retire). This is especially important for those with chronic health or on-going physical limitations. This could be a major cost in your retirement so it's important to determine the options available to you including funding it yourself instead of insurance. Attending one or more retirement workshops in your middle years allows you to think long term. Too many teachers wait until their final five years to understand how their pension works. Don't get caught off guard with assumptions you were making all those years only to discover you were wrong. Plus as you know from my introduction, there is usually free food and door prizes!

For those who are afraid of retirement and don't know what to do with themselves when they aren't working, try a deferred leave of six months or a year. If you've read your CBA (see Strategy 2 in chapter one), you will know if you are eligible for a deferred leave (sabbatical). This differs from a leave-of-absence or maternity/parental leave. A deferred leave is a special agreement between your employer, yourself and the Canada Revenue Agency. It allows your salary of x years to be spread out over y years. For example, the first one I did was a four-over-five. I worked for four years where 25% of my pay was deducted and saved by my district. The fifth year of the plan, I had fourteen months off (two summers sandwiched the school year), my job was held for me upon return and I was paid the salary saved for me over the previous four years (plus the interest earned at the end of my leave). The contract stipulated that I had to return to my job for at least the same period I was released (i.e. one school year). The CRA recognized my lower tax bracket for the five years, the pension board credited me with a year and recognized my higher salary rate (even though I technically did not work) as I kept paying into my pension and, I had the opportunity to travel, work in a different field (ESL instructor in Europe and Central America) and re-energize to reintegrate back to my job. I was single the first time I took my sabbatical year and paid my own benefits (which were subtracted from my bi-weekly pay). I decided during my second sabbatical (a three-over-four) to not pay for benefits and paid for travel insurance and medication out of pocket. I forewent massages and dental check-ups until I returned to my work. These are all personal decisions that you should determine for yourself. A sabbatical could be a great way to test your retirement passion bucket. Is it all you expected or are you bored? Good to know when you still have plenty of time before your retire.

There used to be a non-profit program that permitted teacher exchanges and Canadian teachers swapped places with teachers from other countries, many from Australia. Unfortunately, the CEEF ceased to exist as of 2019. You may wish to search the internet for any current programs that help facilitate an exchange, however, without this former organization's structure, it will be a lot more difficult to keep getting paid by your school board while swapping places in another country. There are opportunities to teach for the Department of National Defence (DND) in Europe, especially if you are bilingual. The postings are typically two years and are advertised typically one school year in advance. A guest on the *85 After School* podcast shared his experience working in Europe for a DND school. But remember, you want to make sure that the experience falls within your long-term plans and that it doesn't necessarily end up costing you more than you can afford.

Whether you take a maternity leave or a leave-of-absence (not a deferred leave), you won't be paid by your employer, so it is important to understand the impact on your pension. Majority of teachers are women and we tend to have children early in our career, it may feel financially difficult to buy-back your pension for the year of maternity leave. Access your pension estimates online and see the difference it makes to buyback your pension. I bought back two years using RRSP money that I had already personally invested, so it wasn't directly out of pocket. It was more advantageous for me to invest into my teacher pension then to keep hoping the market would produce the same outcome in my RRSP account. I did the risk analysis with my financial planner and he showed me the numbers comparing how the buyback would boost my pension (guarantee) versus keeping it in my RRSP account. You would be wise to do the preliminary work and then seek financial advice to determine what is best for you. There is typically an expiration date on when you can no longer buyback that year of absence. Know the details so you are in control and make the best decision for you.

We know that we build wealth by accumulating assets over liabilities. You often hear that a mortgage is "good" debt versus carrying a balance on your credit card is "bad" debt. Although that is true, debt is debt. You will have to learn to prioritize where your money goes to but try not to take on any more debt than you already have. You accumulate wealth by building equity in your home the longer you stay put. If you don't have a reason to move, focus on paying off your mortgage. I know everyone has house envy but really consider whether it is a want or a need. You can always acquire a second property if you want to make passive income. These types of investments are often encouraged for those who have high job-security, like teachers. Do your research, determine if you have the personality for being a landlord and investigate fully what the financial gains and risks could be for your situation. Again, it's a personal decision given your lifestyle and family situation but you build your wealth with less debt, and that includes lessening your mortgage debt.

Summing Up The Middle Years

The middle years are a time of salary increases, job security, honing skills and working smarter not harder. It is also a time to determine if you wish to pursue the ladder of educational leadership, pivot or, develop post-career passions all while building your wealth portfolio. Expanding your network beyond teacher professionals will provide varying insights and perspectives that will help you reflect and determine your career pathway. Most of all, nurturing passions and exploring them now is key to a smooth transition post-career. Don't say "I'll wait till retirement" as you never know if you can still do it given your physical ability, state of being or changing interest. The best discovery is finding out you dislike something now that you thought you would commit to in retirement. Everyone speaks of golf, but if you don't play it now, who says you'll either be able to or even like it when you retire? And even if it is your passion, you can't play golf every day of the year. What else is filling your passion bucket? Use the stable middle-years of your career to cultivate those passions that bring you joy beyond teaching.

CHAPTER THREE

The Later, Senior Years

Your career has been fulfilling, varied and you are both elated and exhausted. But you're hanging in there because you've only got a dozen years or so to go. At this point you've completed more years than you have left. You are in the senior stretch of your teaching career. You may have already secured a leadership position that has boosted your income and you are aiming to go further so that you can maximize your salary in the last five years (which we will discuss in the next chapter). You have sought and obtained credentials that have elevated you in pay and status. In all accounts you are enjoying your career, even with its challenges. Hopefully, your life-work balance is a priority. If you feel consumed by your work and you find yourself placing your other passions on the back burner it may be time to re-examine and make some worthwhile lifestyle changes. In these later years of your career you're intensifying your commitment to several areas that beginning and middle-career teachers have only started to explore and become familiar with in their experience.

Commitment 1:

Educational Leadership Position

If your focus in the middle years was to become a principal or other educational leader, be sure that you are now applying or seeking out these opportunities if you have not yet moved to these positions. If the competition is fierce and you don't make it the first time, be sure to receive constructive feedback that will provide you with either a pathway to gaining further credentials required or more experiences to scaffold your leadership formation. Do not be afraid to apply to leadership positions where you may be lacking one or two skills. Others who do not apply because they feel that way will never know if they could've had a real chance or not. Informal and voluntary leadership positions allow you to gain experience and provide you with real examples during interviews or for inclusion in your portfolio.

Look for additional leadership opportunities even if they are short-term. Many committees require a Chair to lead the group. Your district may be engaged in a strategic plan review and require input from stakeholders. Although people wish to be members of a committee, they may fear the assumed-responsibility of being the leader. If you don't know anything about chairing a meeting, this can be easily learned. Your association probably has a learning session (for free) on how to Chair meetings or about parliamentary rules. You have taught groups of varying students, attended workshops and other meetings so you are familiar with aspects of what makes a functional and dysfunctional meeting. Your years of leading clubs or groups at the school level have helped you organize, plan and execute projects. Channel those skills into leading adults. Adults may challenge you differently than children or youth but if you have a sound understanding of attentive listening and effective communication skills (like the diplomacy you developed during parent-teacher interviews) you are more than capable of chairing a meeting.

Perhaps your subject association or professional organization requires volunteers for a short-term project that eventually may lead to a full-time position that with your experience and connections would make you a strong candidate.   It isn't unheard of that administrators or principals working for a district successfully transfer to a job at the Ministry of Education either for a specific project or for full-time opening. Similarly, some of the provincial union positions are coveted because of the high salary, benefits and continuation in the teachers' pension.

Keep adding to your experiences and refresh your portfolio every couple of years so that it is ready to go when job postings occur or opportunities require you to submit a resumé within a short timeframe. It would be wise, knowing who you would like to have as references, to ask those individuals if they agree to herald your accomplishments and strengths either verbally or in written format. You may even have a couple of points you'd like them to highlight or don't be surprised if they tell you to draft a letter that they can review and sign. So be prepared. This leaves out the pressure of scrambling when it comes time to submit an application. All in all you are well on your way to climb the educational leadership ladder, you have to be prepared to try, not be afraid to fail, and push forward with your determination.

This first Commitment really focuses on those who have chosen to move up the leadership ladder but I know not all of you decided to follow that pathway.   You will recall from Focus 2 in the previous chapter that there are many alternatives if you opt out of moving through the educational ranks.   The senior years are really about intensifying your commitment to your Focus 2 passion. Perhaps your side hustle has built momentum and opened up opportunities that weren't even on your radar when your first began to pursue it.   You are committed to expanding your brand, influence and recognition that increases additional income that you may be earning. Don't be afraid to work on your side hustle. Many teachers may feel the need to hide a successful small business they work at parallel to their teaching job.   There may seem to be an unwritten code amongst teachers that you're not as dedicated when you are passionate about your small business or side hustle. Don't listen to the critics. Don't feel shame in being able to balance your teaching job and another career. Instead take pride in your amazing capacity to balance work with life and your passions. Secretly others wish to be as confident and successful.

Commitment 2:

Networking

We all have our work friends that we so enjoy spending those precious minutes with during a chaotic school day. When you think about it, teaching can be a very isolating job. You have the option of closing your door and spending the entire day just interacting with your students. However, that would not be good for your students or for you as a professional. Networking with colleagues is more than interacting with them at school, as you well know. In these later years of your career you have made connections and know many colleagues not just in your school but hopefully in other schools in the district.   Moreover, by now you've had the opportunity to grow connections, whether in person or online, with professionals outside of the education realm that compliment the work you do on a daily basis but also for future passions you wish to pursue post-career.

It is advisable, with all your skills, knowledge and experience, that you work with new talent. This may be formal mentoring or working on a project with a diverse group of beginning teachers. When you interact with beginning teachers you will learn the theories they have been exposed to by educational researchers at the Faculty of Education. Yes, it is true that some of those theories do not translate effectively into practice but having the ideas presented by an enthusiastic beginning teacher (you once were one) will not only reignite your curiosity for learning but you will also be able to share your experiences. When you retire, you will still have a network of individuals working full-time with whom you can connect.

Some of the most supportive contacts I made in my network weren't even in the education sector. I learned so much from participating in the PSW Programme Review Committee at a local college when I was invited to be a committee member. I connected with social workers and psychologists whom I could brainstorm with when encountering difficult situations with students. Of course these conversations were at a high level and never revealed any confidentiality or details of the student but it allowed for discussions that added to my knowledge and understanding outside of my field.

Coincidentally, connecting online with a business owner who first lived in Edmonton then moved with her family to Spain and, who had attended the same university as me, offered me an opportunity to collaborate and work with her for a summer in Andalucia.

Networking is especially valuable if you already know what fills your passion bucket now and which you wish to pursue in retirement. It is easier to build a network over a longer period of time than starting from scratch in retirement when your professional interactions drastically diminish. Hence, if you love pottery and see yourself building a small business offering pottery classes once you retire from teaching, have you connected with artists? Are you following potters on socials to see their creations? Are you building your brand by promoting yourself and working your way into those networks? It is always better to be in a community than wishing you were part of it. It may take some effort but over several years, it is easier to do than in a short amount of time when needed.

Commitment 3:

Know Your Net Worth and Continue Building Your Wealth

In the more senior years, teaching fatigue kicks in or a health concern may occur that you were not expecting. You may wish to re-read Focus 3 of Chapter 2 regarding deferred leave opportunities. As teachers, we are fortunate that our benefits do provide sick leaves while still receiving compensation. In our senior years we are also earning a better paycheque and hopefully have curtailed our debt. Young children are now teenagers or headed off to university and, while they still cost money, we can see the end of the tunnel for them to move on to start supporting themselves.

If in your senior teaching years you have never engaged in financial and personal goal setting[14], this is really the time to learn more about it. Chapter 4 also delves a bit deeper into goal setting. If you have investments with a company or bank, you can access a financial planner to develop a plan to map out the lifestyle you wish to live in retirement. This usually starts by calculating your net worth by listing your assets and liabilities.

For example, whether you're single or coupled, do you know your monthly expenses? How much money do you need to pay for basic needs like housing, electricity, car loan, insurance, groceries, phone and the like in a year? If you've never done this exercise, I would highly recommend you start it now so you can understand how much you need once you retire, just to live. You can find a template to record basic needs in Appendix 2. Then use the pension calculator available on the teachers' pension website to determine the estimate of your pension in various scenarios (i.e. full pension, retire early). This will help you see if there is a gap between what you need to pay for basic living and the monthly pension you are expected to receive. If you see there is a gap, you need to make sure your supplemental investments are going to help cover it or you will need to adjust your lifestyle expectations accordingly. Also, you will recall from the previous chapter, in Focus 3, you should determine if buying back a leave-of-absence or maternity leave is favourable, if that applies to you. Your pension is one of your largest assets so it would be wise to run the scenarios of buying back versus investing it elsewhere. This is where a financial plan can really help you determine the estimated growth of your investments aside from your pension.

Furthermore, you want to make sure that you are keenly aware of what your net worth is at least ten and five years prior to retiring. This is important because you are at your most desirable (to banks at least) when you are a high earner and have a strong net worth. This will allow you to secure a line of credit based on your salary, which will remain as long as you keep it post-retirement. Applying for a line of credit in retirement based on your pension salary may not be as advantageous. You may never even use it, but the security of having it, at really no cost to you (unless used), is worth the effort. Again, I am not a financial planner or advisor, so you are encouraged to speak to a certified professional to determine your own personalized financial plan. You can also do the preliminary work of calculating your net worth by using online calculators[15].

Perhaps you've found the time and energy to succeed in a side hustle that you hope to turn into a full-fledged gig once you retire or leave teaching. This is not only a great way to add more to your investments but also to understand the tax advantages of running a small business in your own home. For example, I know many teachers who have taught college or university courses to in-service and pre-service teachers that were hired as independent contractors. It would be smart to ask an accountant what you may be eligible for in tax credits or deductions given your work-from-home situation.

The simple instruction, but difficult task to execute, is to reduce your debt, live below your earnings and make solid investment choices that match your risk-tolerance. I once worked with a teacher who had five to seven years left before retirement. He loved trading penny stocks and it became not only a hobby for him, but a sport to determine what he'd buy, hold and sell at a profit. Eventually he felt he had the skills and knowledge to leave teaching and become a day trader. I regret not staying in touch with him once he left, as I'd be curious to know how his next chapter helped him build further wealth beyond his teachers' pension and other investments. Regardless, he was a sound believer that building wealth was about determining your risk tolerance and knowing what you're investing in before spending your hard earned money.

Summing Up the Later, Senior Years

The senior years are all about revelling in how much we've grown over the years in our professional aspirations. We may be in a leadership position where we are enjoying both the challenge and interactions with new colleagues. With only a dozen or less years to go to full retirement, we can see the light at the end of the tunnel but we are still enjoying the daily grind. Perhaps we determined that educational leadership wasn't our way of maximizing our earning potential and we decided that a side hustle or small business in addition to our full-time job was more gratifying. All in all, the goal is to network with our colleagues and join communities that support our interests post-teaching. Networking not only keeps us connected once we retire or pivot, it is also much easier to keep abreast of the latest trends and discoveries in teaching or interest of your choice. Staying connected is not only good for our social wellbeing but also is reciprocal to our undertakings in retirement. Knowing our net worth and what our financial plan is in the ten and five years before retirement will help us accelerate our savings and investment goals. If you already know from your financial plan that you're going to need ten thousand dollars more per year than what your pension is predicted to provide, then you know that you either work longer, have to bank on other investments or income, or reduce your expenditures in retirement. As teachers we are trained to do daily, unit and long-term planning. Use those skills to help you set your personal and financial goals[16] in your senior years.

CHAPTER FOUR

The Last Five Years

Can you believe it? It feels like yesterday when you started in a classroom with thirty students in your charge. You only have five years left to reach that magical moment where a full pension is yours. You have been doing all the legwork over the course of your career and you know what your vision and plan is for the life you want post-teaching.   How far you have come! If you haven't read the previous chapter, it will be beneficial to read it first, specifically Commitment 3. Even if you just started to really plan your personal and financial goals, you still have five years to make your vision a reality. This chapter focuses on the essential planning steps in the last five years of your teaching career. Tailor them to fit the retirement you want.

Step 1: Reach the Next Level in Leadership

Again, some of you have moved through the leadership ladder in education. That could mean you're ready to go from principal to superintendent or director. It could also mean you are ready to be union president, or move up to a Ministry job. For those who did not veer into the path of educational leadership but established a side hustle that compliments their teaching role, you are still seeking opportunities to reach the expert, leadership level in both your teaching role and secondary job. I know that not all the opportunities may present themselves in your immediate geographic area, but realize that post-pandemic, the world is much more flexible in how we work. In upper leadership, you motivate the teams with your vision of the strategic plan that is to be carried out. You are creative and experienced enough to know how to make your work-life balance with your home-life even if there is extended commutes or separation time-requirements.

I worked with an upper executive in a school board who was offered the top job approximately 300 km away. Her entire family was well established in our geographic area but instead of agonizing over whether or not to take the job and move, she and her partner decided she would take the job for the three-year contract and commute on weekends and make her schedule flexible enough so that remote work was included. After the three years, although it was exhausting at times, she added another three years to her contract before finally moving into retirement. The stage of her career, the grown family that she was no longer directly responsible for and a supportive partner all meshed to make this workable for her.

Another colleague decided to take an educational leadership role about a three-hour train ride from her century home that she loved. With a significant pay raise, she was able to pay rent in shared accommodations in the new job location.   There was also the opportunity for remote work and her job did require her to travel throughout the province, leaving her with a flexible schedule beyond our typical 8 to 4 school day (where the bell dictates our bio-breaks). This flexibility allowed her to claim weekdays as her weekend because of travel time used on a Saturday or Sunday.

These are individual examples but in the grand scheme of things, when you are in the last five years of your career, you want to reach the highest leadership level not only for personal achievement but also to maximize your income.

Step 2: Maximize Your Income and Benefits

Most defined-benefit pension plans work on the idea of your average best-five years. Typically, the last five-years of your teaching career, due to presumed raises provided by contract negotiations, will be your highest. If you've reached the executive level of leadership, you will also have many other benefits as part of your contract. Many teachers early in their career may be unaware of the extra perks that leadership roles provide, but even though these career pathways are in the public sector (without corporate bonuses), there are benefits. In executive-leadership careers you are expected to lead your organization and this requires networking, travel and involvement in various associations. Your employer typically covers these costs. I know of executive union leaders whose contract negotiations include a housing allowance, wardrobe allowance, dining and entertainment allowance, and probably some other perks. Once you reach the upper levels of leadership, especially if you are no longer technically in the public sector (i.e. not working for a school board) but still able to contribute to your provincial teacher pension plan, you can definitely maximize your income and benefits.

This is also a time to reflect on your health needs. If you require surgery or extensive dental work (because we all get older), this is the time to determine if you are going to do this while still working for two reasons: you have health coverage and you have access to sick leave. It will be up to you to research if you actually require coverage in retirement or if you will pay out of pocket. I did the math for myself and it was not beneficial for me to insure myself in retirement as I am healthy and pay out of pocket for my medication and dental check-ups. Even with those costs, I'm still below the annual cost of buying insurance. However, I know colleagues who are still working, even though they are eligible to retire, because they know that either no insurance company will take them on or the out-of-pocket costs of medication for their partner or dependent-child is not affordable. You're in your last five years of your career. Use the time to research the plans offered specifically for teachers or larger private plans that are advertised through insurance companies.

You're An Expert, Ca$h in on that!

You have decades of experience working with children, youth and even adults (colleagues are a special group), so make that work for you. What is your area of expertise that you've been working on throughout your career: special education, early literacy, wellness, physical education, or leadership skills? Perhaps it is something more niche like social-justice curriculum connections. At this stage you probably have not only intellectual property but also physical resources that would help those in the early and middle stages of their career. There are many sites where teachers sell their resources at an affordable cost. If you are more inclined to pay it forward, you can still upload your resources for free or suggest a donation to a favourite charity. Likewise, there are organizations that are always looking for expert practitioners to share their knowledge whether at a conference, webinar, panel discussion or part of an association. Many associations or organizations offer honorariums or gifts for your leadership or participation. And if you are in a leadership position, you may be attending these conferences sponsored by your employer. The global connections made through the internet provides a wide audience for you to brand your expertise.

Alternatively, your expertise may be that passion that you've nurtured and developed parallel to your teaching career. That expertise may have a very receptive audience with your teacher colleagues. I know one teacher who, for example, was super comfortable doing her own taxes, bypassing the pop-up services that seemed to overcharge around the tax season. Word got around and although her disclaimer has always been that she is not a professional accountant and that everyone is still responsible for ensuring accuracy, she started assisting many other teachers because she had sharpened her expertise in using the software. The point is, we as teachers, by nature, tend to give away our expertise and service for free: I don't know lawyers, dentists, or doctors who give away their expertise as freely. So, don't feel guilty about monetizing your expertise. If you want to tutor (students other than those at your school to avoid conflict of interest) because you enjoy the work with individual or small groups of learners, don't feel guilty about charging your worth. You are an expert, and you have a right to cash in on that.

Step 3: Conscientious Retirement Planning

If you have not already followed the suggestions in the previous chapter's Commitment 3, in particular, reflecting on your personal and financial goals, I suggest you take time to do that now. This is a great time to do an inventory of your net worth and your personal goals: what you are retiring to, not from?

Let's start with your personal goals. Do you know what will fill your days when you retire? Many are excited to travel, play golf or sport of choice and spend time with grandchildren. These are all wonderful endeavours but they won't fill each and every day. Remember when you retire, you do not have a set schedule or structure that your work dictates. Now, teachers have a bit more experience with that than the mainstream given July and August as non-teaching months for most. You know the feeling when we sometimes forget what day of the week it is, but doing it for the entire year is a different story.

Reflect on the following statements or questions and jot down the first thing that comes to mind. Let it sit for a week and come back to it. Change any answers you want and then start making notes on what you need in order to reach your personal goals. Doing this type of exercise in 30-, 60-, or 90-day intervals helps you fine-tune what you're really interested in at your core. For a more in-depth reflection on your personal goals in retirement, see Appendix 3.

1. What dreams did you have when you were younger? Take one minute and make a list of all the things you want (or wanted) to accomplish but don't have time for because of work.

2. Describe what you imagine a typical day in retirement will be like for you.

3. Name the people with whom you can or will be connecting with during the 'work-day' when retired.

4. What types of activities will you pursue with those individuals? What will you pursue on your own? Do any of these activities link back to your list in #1?

5. Finish this statement with the first thoughts that come to mind:
What I will miss the most about teaching/working is… and I plan to… to lessen the feeling of loss.

6. If partnered: my partner and I have discussed our shared and individual goals.
Yes or No

As you can see, this exercise provokes you to think in more tangible ways in how you will be spending your days during early retirement. Having the day to yourself to plan as you wish is a freedom that might need a bit more structure than expected. This, for some, is a bigger adjustment than expected. Taking the time to brainstorm, reflect and revisit such inventories is a great starting point for conscientiously planning your personal goals.

If you attend any retirement workshops, there may be similar inventories recommended but rarely do they delve deeper to provide you with a feeling that you know what you're retiring to. Typically those workshops only focus on the immediate years after retirement even though there are typically three phases. The first phase is the most active when retirees tend to spend the most money. This is the age-cohort when retirees wish to travel, join various organizations where memberships may be required, still support adult-children who are starting out in their careers and having children, or even start a small business. Retirees in this first phase generally are healthy, mobile and very independent. The second phase of retirement, commences perhaps as much as 15 or 20 years in, tends to see a slow down of travel, perhaps less expenditure on adult-children and family, a reduction in the number of activities that require membership fees, and perhaps a reduction in daily living costs as well. The third phase, one we do not wish to occur until we are much older, is the stability phase where our daily lives are much slower than what it was when we were in our sixties and seventies. We may experience chronic health issues and our mobility may decline as we age. This may also create an increase in expenses for health-care related services. Our interests may narrow depending on how involved we stay with our intergenerational connections. We may also experience loss of friends, further shrinking our social network. This phase for many seems too far away to think about when on the brink of retirement. It may even seem like you do not have to plan for that phase at this moment. However, long-term estate planning and making sure your loved ones know what your wishes are (like staying in your own home or moving to a retirement home) is something you probably want to think about when you feel the shift from phase two to three coming. That way you know what the options are when you need it in the third phase.

If you think about the three phases, it will be much easier to permit yourself to set personal goals for the first phase so that you have no regrets about fulfilling them. You should also give yourself permission to change your goals if what you thought would be your focus turns out to disappoint. Plus you owe no one an explanation and there is no shame in changing your mind. After all, you are in control and you get to decide what you want to do and accomplish. Sometimes it is as simple as learning how to swim because you never had the time or encouragement to do so when you were busy working and raising a family. Other times it is as ambitious as writing a book and publishing it because… you never had the time or encouragement to do so when you were busy working. You get the idea. If you wish to have more guidance in exploring your personal goals join our online community on Facebook or Instagram at *85 After School*.

Once you know what your personal goals are, it is time to determine how your pension, investments and savings will pay for all your plans. The Ontario Teachers' Pension Plan reports[17] that the average pension paid in 2023 is $50,000.   You should take an inventory of your wealth, determine your expenses and create a budget that will help you through the phases of retirement. There are many resources online that will help you through this process, however, we will start with the basics.

First, make a basic list of all your assets and debt. This is a simple list of all the assets you own (e.g. house, car, investments, pension etc.) and the debt you have (e.g. mortgage, loans, credit card balance etc.). This will allow you to see the big picture of where you stand regarding your net worth. Simply subtract what you owe from what you own and you will see if you are in the positive or negative standing. Hopefully, it is positive and at or above the Canadian average. If you want to go in a bit more depth, then use an online net-worth calculator. Next, write a list of all your monthly obligations that you have to pay: utility bills, car payments, mortgage, groceries, memberships etc. If you're not a budgeter (most people are not), don't forget to factor in non-regular payments such as property tax, insurance or travel/vacation expenditures. Simply divide what you spent last year on travel by 12 months and you'll know the monthly budget line. Then add up what you spend on a monthly basis just to 'live' the way you 'live' now. You already know that most pension plans allow you to run personalized scenarios to determine the amount of income you can expect (showing you both gross and net annual pension payments). How does your monthly expenditures measure up to the annual pension you are estimated to receive? Generally, costs such as gas for commuting and clothing purchases will greatly reduce in retirement. The exercise of calculating your net worth and determining your monthly expenses will give you a starting point to determine where there may be shortfalls and how to adjust accordingly. Again, it would be best to discuss your financial goals with a professional who is licensed to provide you with expert advice.

Step 4: Determine Your Needs for a Financial and/or Estate Planner

If you feel your circumstances, net worth or partnership is more complicated than you can handle yourself, a financial planner or estate planner can assist. I will not go into detail about what these professionals can offer you, as I am not a financial nor a legal expert. However, from my own experience, I have found it helpful to work with a financial planner who has run personalized financial plans given certain assumptions so that I had a better understanding of my own situation. It also helped me decide what to invest in using the various vehicles available to Canadians (e.g. RRSP, TSFA, stock market, mutual funds etc.).   Through your current employer, if you have access to EAP (Employee Assistance Program), you may be able to receive retirement counselling and/or planning. Each employer's EAP is different. If you've never accessed it, connect with them and see if this service is available to you. By attending your pension sponsor or union's free retirement workshops, you may also gain insight to accessing such experts.   I know in Ontario, there is a corporation focused on providing investment services just for educators. In the past they have offered a free first-session with a Certified Financial Planner to gain potential clients. You should do your due-diligence and determine what is right for you. If you do work with an expert, it is customary to consult and meet with them at least once a year. When you are in your last five years you will probably be in more frequent contact and have them run an up-to-date financial plan for you. Perhaps you are very skilled in managing your own investments and have no need for a financial planner or estate planner. In that case, congratulations! Most of us need at least a little help from an expert.

Step 5: From Conscientious Planning to Laying the Groundwork for A Successful Transition

In Step 3 you completed an inventory of your personal retirement goals. A week later you revisited the list of goals that you brainstormed and identified the passions that would keep you engaged in the first five years. For some that might be travel. For others it could be crafts, volunteering or even working part-time. Whatever your aspirations may be this is the time, in the last five years of your full-time teaching career, to lay the groundwork for a successful transition.

Do you need to learn a skill or refine a skill for the goals you have listed? If so, this is the time you can still receive funding from various sources in the education sector. You have many contacts in your network, be sure to maintain and enhance your connections. Eventually you will be leaving the daily grind and access to those still working decreases because you will not see them at the same intervals or intensity you did while working. Keep that in mind. You will have more time but they won't. Remember they are still in the trenches working and as much as they would love to help, their priorities are not the same as yours when you're retired. That is why it is helpful to have a large network of intergenerational professionals from all walks of life. Work on building your brand and network so that the ripple effect will continue well into retirement.

If you have your sights set on substitute/supply teaching once you retire, be sure to have an updated resumé. Even if you are planning on being hired by your former employer, you are still required to update your resumé. Furthermore, if there is a high demand for educators, you may benefit from working for multiple employers and making yourself available for alternative assignments. While you're still working and you're thinking of perhaps moving to another jurisdiction where you are required to have a teaching license, go through the credentialing process in the last couple of years of your full-time employment. The credentialing process in some jurisdictions may require you to send attestations from a current employer and that is much easier when you're still working than when you're retired. Read more about licensing in other jurisdictions in Chapter 6. This also pertains to other types of teaching credentials such as TEFL (teaching English as a foreign language). Might as well finish that certification while you are still working to take advantage of any funding that may be available to you as a full-time educator. Many of these credentials are helpful if one of your goals is to work as an educator abroad once you retire.

There may be other skills that you wish to develop or perfect during your last years of full-time employment so that you can smoothly transition to accomplishing your retirement goals. I started intensively learning French about five years before retiring. My purpose was mostly personal interest (I love languages) but also considered that, in Canada, being bilingual in the official languages provides opportunities. Every year I review my five- and ten-year personal and financial goals (I am a type A person so this is right up my alley) and part of the plan was to advance my proficiency in French, become a better tennis player, become physically stronger to accomplish some challenging hikes and ensure I had saved sufficiently for a travel fund in retirement that allowed for at least two annual trips. Learning French really paid off, not just as a personal goal, but more so in my daily life now living in Québec.   As for tennis, I have hope I will improve but it sure is fun working towards that goal (it is about the journey). And – I hope to conquer Mount Kilimanjaro next year! If you are pushing something off until retirement, reflect back to your list of personal goals and see if there are building blocks that need to be put in place now in order to smoothly transition when that retirement date finally arrives.

Summing Up the Last Five Years

I once heard a wiser and more senior teacher compare life to a toilet paper roll: it spins faster the closer you get to the end.   At twenty-five I merely gave a polite laugh.   It was funny but it didn't mean anything to me.   As I got older (and wiser) I started to really grasp that concept.   I think life seems to fly by for several reasons. First, you are engaged or passionate about what you are doing, whether that is teaching or the other passions you are pursuing in parallel.   As you get older, your reference of time is much different. We also slow down. We are not as quick as the newly hired, fresh-out-of-the-faculty teachers. You may be an exception but I'm speaking in generalities or perhaps just about me.   I notice this with my intergenerational interactions, in comparison I am not as quick as they are or as I used to be. But where I may have diminished in speed, I have gained experience and insight that balances well for the same productivity as my younger counterparts.   I often thought

Kindergarten should be left to the younger teachers (I know, ageism at its best) because the children are young and energetic but a master teacher has gone through all the cycles and fads of education, and skilfully facilitates learning for those students. Which reminds me of a kindergarten teacher in my previous School Board who finally retired at age 71. She had waited until her daughter, also a teacher, retired early.

Your last five years are a time to see the finish line and prepare. Aim for the highest rank of educational leadership if that is the path you have chosen. Increase your income and maximize your benefits. Remember your expertise can be monetized in addition to your regular income. If that is of interest to you and you are willing to put in some extra time, it will pay off. Take the time to consciously plan your retirement. You should go to the workshops (try more than one, there is always something new to be learned). Take inventory of your personal goals; your passions that you wish to pursue in retirement. Likewise, the deliberate activity of understanding your financial situation (fixed expenses, your assets and liabilities) will show you the big picture of what will be doable and affordable in retirement. Determine if you would benefit from the services of a financial planner or estate planner. Depending on your situation, whether you are coupled or single, have multiple investments beyond your pension or, are heavily invested in real estate, seek out a professional to provide a financial plan if you want an expert opinion on your situation. Lastly, don't put off conscientiously planning for your transition into retirement. Step 5 in this chapter is the grunt work and you should schedule it in your calendar just as you would parent-teacher interviews. The five years you have left will fly by and it'll be like the end of that toilet paper roll.

Part 2

Reinvention and Moving On

CHAPTER FIVE

Pivot or Alternatives

At some point in your teaching career, you may be thinking you want to leave as the job is too stressful and work-life balance isn't what you want it to be or you simply know that teaching is not for you. This is not an uncommon thought or feeling. What do you do when that happens? There are three easy steps to determine if pivoting or seeking alternatives is your path to a more satisfying career or lifestyle.

Step 1: Examine the Pros and Cons

It would be unwise to just quit in a state of stress when you are not satisfied with how your career or life is unfolding. If you need to step away you have access to medical leave or unpaid leave-of-absence while job security continues. As I stated in Chapter 1, if you really don't enjoy working in education, don't stay for the pension or benefits. Your life is worth so much more than that and you could have a much more satisfying career when you are passionate or enjoying the 40 hours or more you work a week. So start by making a list of pros and cons about the current job you are doing in education. You can then look at each of the points you have listed and assign them a value in relation to how much you detest (for the con) and how much you love (for the pros) each point. If it's difficult for you to list concrete pros and cons, ask yourself the following questions instead:

1.   Do you feel disconnected from the work you do in your classroom?

2.   Do you feel disappointed by what you thought the job would entail versus what it is?

3.   Do you feel you're treated as a professional or do you feel there is mistrust in your work environment?

4.   Do you have moments of joy or satisfaction at least once a week?

5.   Do you feel like you are connected to the people with whom you work and working towards shared goals?

6.   Are you happy at least sometimes at work?

7.   Are you compromising your personal life for work?

8.   Do you feel unsafe or unappreciated most of the time at work?

9. Do you feel your skills are mismatched with what you are required to do daily?

10. What three things would make daily work at least a bit better? Do you have the power to change it?

Obviously there are no right or wrong answers to these questions. The purpose is to examine and reflect on whether or not it is time for a change. Quiet contemplation when your feelings are neutral (not after a particularly tough day) is key to really exploring your state of being. This will give you an idea of whether you are in a temporary slump or whether this is a deeper feeling of needing a career change. As mentioned in Step 4 of Chapter 4, you may also have access to counselling through your EAP to help you determine the root of your dissatisfaction. Again, no one can give you the answer. The answer lies within you. Examining the pros and cons of your job and reflecting deeply on how you envision your career to unfold is the first step in deciding whether to pivot from teaching or finding alternatives.

Step 2: Research Options Available
If you have reflected and really are leaning towards wanting to pivot from a career in education, you are probably wondering what are the options. If you know exactly what you want to do, you are well on your way to making the change. You have most likely already invested much of your non-work time thinking about how to make the change tangible. Still prepare and research so your transition will be as successful as possible. For those who aren't sure what options are out there, let's take some time to reflect. Before you read a sample list

of alternative careers, make an inventory of all the skills you have based on your work experience to-date. For example, planning and designing learning activities based on curriculum expectations (a requirement of the job) highlight your ability to organize, design, develop, as well as, execute a plan. Being able to keep thirty children or youth engaged in learning (admittedly at varying degrees), following instructions and, maintaining an orderly environment, demonstrates your management skills. Writing report cards, holding parent-teacher interviews, and providing feedback on assessed work demonstrates your precision in communicating. All these examples are transferable skills to many other service-industry careers. Ask your colleagues what they feel you are really good at and take out the 'educational jargon' to identify the skills which are in demand in other careers. Scroll through the job sites or apps with the list of skills you have identified and you will find many other careers that use your professional skills. Some common sites are: Glassdoor, LinkedIn, or Facebook.

The job site Indeed[18] lists the following careers as popular alternatives to teaching:
- Researcher
- Education Consultant
- Corporate Trainer
- Project Management
- Career Counsellor
- Event Planner
- Childcare Provider
- Real Estate Agent
- Wholesale Manager

- Writer
- Museum Curator
- Human Resource Specialist
- Life Coach

The jobs listed may not be of interest to you at all, so I would suggest that you look at the skills you have and what you really enjoy doing. Then search by skill-based careers and discover if there are any credentials required before being considered for such positions. For example, if you enjoy creating units of study, instructional design may be the right job for you. As a teacher we do not call it instructional design but since the pandemic, I am sure you have a large depot of e-units that you have designed. YouTube will easily get you up to speed on the lingo used in that sector and what Instructional Designers create. The key here is to really focus on your skillset, knowledge and where your passion lies.

Step 3: Take the Leap

Before you take the leap, think about what you will possibly regret leaving your teaching career. If you are on the verge or close to retirement, there are alternatives. For example, if you want to try another job or spend more time on your business can you afford to take a leave of absence? Most CBAs allow employees to either take a deferred leave (e.g. plan ahead for a 3-over-4) or an unpaid leave of absence, holding your job for you. Perhaps you are at the retirement age but not quite ready to let go. In this case, you may be eligible to drop to part-time work. In Québec, for example, teachers that don't want to quit cold-turkey can sign up for progressive retirement, reducing their workload by a percentage every year. Some take five years to retire fully.

If you are nowhere near retirement but have decided to pivot to your next career here are seven tips[19] to make the transition as smooth as possible:

1.   Make a list of your transferable skills

2.   Choose your intended career direction and goal

3.   Re-write your resumé from scratch, emphasizing all your transferable skills using language and lingo used in your intended career

4.   Connect with recruitment agencies and research job requirements through sites such as LinkedIn, Glassdoor, and Indeed

5.   Rehearse responses to typical questions that would be asked in your intended career

6.   Connect with those in the field and see if (prior to leaving teaching) you can shadow or intern during your summer months

7.   Apply to postings in your intended career to get your foot in the door.

So, if you are confident that you are ready to cut the cord and definitely leave your teaching career, congratulations for being so decisive. It is a difficult decision but you won't regret it because you have reflected in earnest what the next best step is for you. None of the former teachers I mentioned in Chapter 2, Focus 2 have returned to teaching. They are thriving and enjoying their job changes. If you are in a partnership, it may be easier to take the leap. For those supporting themselves, remember that you can take the leap in stages, and eventually let go and never look back.

Summing Up Pivoting from - and Alternatives to - Teaching

Remember you have options in education that will have you leave the classroom but not necessarily the sector. You may wish to become a consultant, administrator or executive in an educational association. However, if you want to leap from the education sector and pursue a completely different job or career, you have many transferable skills that are highly sought after. Start by examining the pros and cons of leaving your teaching career. You may need some neutral outside support in order to fairly examine your thoughts and feelings about pivoting. For many it is an exciting and welcomed opportunity. Next, research options available. This is one of the most important steps because you don't want to pivot with rose-coloured glasses and regret your decision. Once you have made the decision to pivot, remember you can do it in stages. If you are at the end of your teaching career and are ready to pivot to something else, you have less pressure than those who may be in the middle-years of their career. Regardless, you have planned it and you are ready. Enjoy it.

CHAPTER SIX

Licensing in Other Jurisdictions

In Canada, if you are a licensed teacher in one province, the Canadian Free Trade Agreement permits you to become licensed in other provinces and territories. The Agreement states:

> Labour Mobility provisions of the CFTA (Chapter 7) state that certified workers have to be recognized as qualified to work by a regulatory body in another province or territory which regulates that occupation, without having to go through significant additional training, work experience, examination or assessment, unless an exception has been posted. (Labour Mobility, https://www.cfta-alec.ca/labour-mobility/)

The exceptions do not affect the teaching profession, hence, it should be straightforward to apply for licensure if you plan on moving to another province and perhaps want to continue teaching full-time or substitute. A retired Ontario teacher can work full-time in another province without it affecting their pension payments. In order to be licensed in another province, you just need patience, as the process can be quite slow. I am originally certified to teach in Ontario, which has a regulatory body. In 2019, after a year-long process, I was provided an Interim Professional Certificate in Alberta from the Ministry of Education. Alberta has since created a public registry that lists all teachers and teacher leaders that have ever held a license in the province. In Québec, it is the Ministry of Education who reviewed my dossier and provided my permanent license called Brevet d'enseignement. I went through the certification process in England (which was by far the easiest experience) and the Netherlands (a bit more constrictive since my training is in English) where I am permitted to work in international schools.

Maintain an electronic portfolio of your original documents that support your application. Typically this includes your degree transcript(s), your initial licence, employment history, copies of government issued identification, and proof of Canadian residency or citizenship. The following chart outlines basic information to help you get started on seeking licensing in other provinces or territories. Best to always check the websites for the most current information.

Province/ Territory[20]	Contact Information and Highlights
British Columbia	There no longer is an independent professional regulator in BC. The Regulatory Branch of the Ministry of Education is responsible for certification and licensing. You can use the tool to discover which certificate you should apply for. https://teacherregulation.gov.bc.ca/Tools/ApplicationSelection/Index.aspx Or you can create an account to start the application process. https://www.bceid.ca/register/basic/account_details.aspx?type=regular The cost is approximately $245 if you completed your teacher training at a Canadian University. General Inquiries: https://www2.gov.bc.ca/gov/content/education-training/k-12/teach/become-a-teacher

Alberta	There is no professional regulator. The Ministry of Education is responsible for certification and licensing. You will need to create a TWINS account where you upload all your documentation and pay your application fee. https://extranet.education.alberta.ca/twins.public/public/ The cost is approximately $225 if you completed your teacher training at a Canadian (non-Alberta) university. General Inquiries: https://www.alberta.ca/teacher-certification#jumplinks-0

Saskatchewan	In 2015, the Saskatchewan Professional Teachers Regulatory Board was established. The regulator is responsible for certification and licensing. The general guidelines for application are found here: https://sptrb.ca//SPTRB/Certification/Canadian%20and%20United%20States%20Teacher's%20Certificate%20Holder.aspx The cost is approximately $216 if you completed teacher training in Canada. And you can start your online application here: https://sptrb.ca/SPTRB/Create_Account/SPTRB/CreateAccount.aspx?hkey=6f5970eb-d07a-4d32-bb6f-810876ca5eae Further general information about the regulator can be found at: https://sptrb.ca/

Manitoba	The Professional Certification Unit is responsible for certification and licensing teachers in Manitoba. The application process is explained here: https://www.edu.gov.mb.ca/k12/profcert/app-process/index.html The cost is approximately $120*-$150[i] for those who have been trained in a non-Manitoban, Canadian University. This fee may be subject to change as per Regulation 86/2010* or what the Ministry of Education[i] has posted. General Inquiries: https://www.edu.gov.mb.ca/k12/profcert/index.html

Ontario	The Ontario College of Teachers is the Professional Regulator that certifies and licenses teachers. You can read the eligibility guidelines, instructions and then apply at the bottom of the following landing page: https://apps.oct.ca/OLR/Template.aspx?action=rege The cost is approximately $140 to register and you pay an annual fee of $200 (subject to change if Council votes in favour of increase or decrease). **General Inquiries:** https://www.oct.ca/~/link.aspx?_id=25CD74DDD6A14F3BA968490666FB1733&_z=z

Québec	There is no professional regulator in Québec. The Ministry of Education is responsible for certification and licensing. The application process does not require a fee. https://prod.education.gouv.qc.ca/formulairewebj/accueil.do?methode=acceder You will need an approved guarantor to authenticate your original documents. General Inquiries: https://www.quebec.ca/en/government/work-government/jobs-education/teaching-general-education-youth-sector-vocational-training-adult-education/obtaining-teaching-licence/types-teaching-licences

New Brunswick	The Ministry of Education through the Education and Early Childhood Department issues certificates and licenses. For teachers trained in Canada (outside of New Brunswick), you must complete Form B: https://www.pxw1.snb.ca/snb7001/e/1000/CSS-FOL-19-002E.pdf The cost is approximately $120. General Inquiries: https://www2.gnb.ca/content/gnb/en/services/services_renderer.599.Teacher_Certification.html

Nova Scotia	The Office of Teacher Certification of the Government's Education and Early Childhood Development department is responsible for licensing teachers. You must create a profile to submit your application. https://teachercertification.novascotia.ca/ A user-guide will help you through the process. http://certification.ednet.ns.ca/sites/default/files/documents/ TCS_New_Applicant_User_Guide_EN.pdf The cost of initial application is approximately $110. General Inquiries: http://certification.ednet.ns.ca/

PEI	The provincial government has assigned a Registrar to certify and license teachers. You will need to apply online to submit your application. https://services.princeedwardisland.ca/en/service/apply-teachers-license-canadian-education-program-outside-pei#/service/GenericWebformSubmission/GenericWebformGenerateTransactionID The cost is approximately $125. There is a two-week turn around in providing you with your teaching license. General Inquiries: https://www.princeedwardisland.ca/en/topic/certification-and-professional-development-for-teachers

| **Newfoundland & Labrador** | The Department of Education is responsible for licensing teachers in the province.

Canadian citizens and permanent residents can apply by completing this form:
https://www.gov.nl.ca/education/files/FormsTeachersCertApplication_FINAL2023-12-04.pdf
Initial applications must be sent by regular post.

You will have to complete the payment form as well. The approximate cost is approximately $115.
https://www.gov.nl.ca/education/files/PaymentSchedule_FINAL2023-07-31.pdf

General Inquiries: https://www.gov.nl.ca/education/k12/teaching/certification/ |

<table>
<tr><td>Nunavut</td><td>

The Department of Education is responsible for licensing teachers.

If you are interested in teaching in Nunavut, contact the Department of Education directly.

info.edu@gov.nu.ca
1 867 975 5600

PO Box 1000, Stn. 900
Iqaluit, NU
X0A 0H0

Or Complete the online contact request:
https://www.gov.nu.ca/en/department-education/contact-us

</td></tr>
</table>

| **NWT** | The Department of Education is responsible for licensing teachers in the territory.

You must create a profile on *CertifiED NWT* in order to request a review of your credentials.
https://gnwt.in1touch.org/index.html

A helpful guide is available to help you with the process.
https://www.ece.gov.nt.ca/sites/ece/files/resources/2022-05_-_fact_sheet_-_certifed_nwt_-_english.pdf

General Inquiries:
https://www.ece.gov.nt.ca/en/services/prospective-teacher-information/teacher-qualification-and-certification |

Yukon	The Department of Education is responsible for issuing a teacher license to qualifying applicants. You can follow the instructions in this uploaded form. https://yukon.ca/sites/yukon.ca/files/edu/edu-teacher-certification-quick-guide-and-document-tracker.pdf Be sure to read the details in relation to how to submit you application and supporting documents. There is an application fee but it is not stated on the website. https://yukon.ca/en/employment/jobs-schools/apply-yukon-teacher-certificate#apply-for-teacher-certification General Inquiries: https://yukon.ca/en/employment/jobs-schools/apply-yukon-teacher-certificate

There are many other jurisdictions that will see Canadian certification as a benefit so it is always a good idea to maintain current should you wish to continue working in education when you retire.   Check NASDTEC to determine the requirements and/or agreements between your province and various States (https://www.nasdtec.net/page/Interstate). As a certified Canadian teacher, you can work in England up to four years without a certificate (called a QTS, qualified teacher status). Create an account and follow the instructions (https://apply-for-qts-in-england.education.gov.uk/teacher/sign_up). Start here to be guided to ensure you qualify (https://apply-for-qts-in-england.education.gov.uk/teacher/sign_in_or_sign_up).

You should be aware that if you hold multiple licenses from various jurisdictions you must adhere to the professional standards of each of the jurisdictions. If you no longer wish to be recognized as being credentialed, some jurisdictions require you to resign with an official letter as opposed to just letting your membership lapse. For this reason, only if you are planning on working in a jurisdiction and being employed in a school that requires official certification should you go through the application process. During a time of high demand for teachers, there may even be an exemption where you begin working prior to completing the certification process. Always check the official websites for updates and current instructions. Several of my colleagues have moved to other jurisdictions, including myself, and have been full-time teachers, administrators or, substitute teachers post-retirement. The information in this chapter supports your journey to become licensed in other jurisdictions.

CHAPTER SEVEN

Reinvention Stories

Imagine that many of you who are contemplating leaving the profession have jumped to this chapter first. I am glad you have. No matter in what order you are reading the book, these are stories that will inspire or resonate with your own experience. The names have been changed and some stories have been simplified to leave out identifying details. In some cases two individual stories have been amalgamated. However, all the stories come from real teachers who have pivoted into a completely different career or became an entrepreneur. You can also listen to the *85 After School* podcast to hear stories from retired teachers following their passions.

From Classroom to Counselling – Monica's Story

I was already a special education consultant at the Board when I met a newly hired teacher by the name of Monica. Monica and another beginning teacher stood out because they accepted all invitations to new learning opportunities. Monica was particularly eager to learn and then implement new strategies in her classroom. In my opinion, she was not only a dedicated teacher but a very astute professional as well. Monica really loved working with the kids and creating a classroom environment that made them want to learn and participate. So you would understand my great surprise when I found out that Monica, about seventeen years into her teaching career, had decided to leave teaching to become a Psychometrist. She had completed her Master's degree in Psychology while teaching full-time and decided that her pathway to help others was better served through private practice. I commend her for following her passion.

Step into the Wild – André's Story

André loved the outdoors. On Mondays he was always sharing his hunting stories or pictures from an amazing sunset in an isolated area that had taken him on a 15-hour hike. In the summer when he wasn't teaching, he'd find his way to an outfitter who'd hire him to lead portaging trips and outdoor adventure trips. He revelled in everything outdoors. Even as he got older and arguably a little less fit than when he was in his twenties, you'd find him sharing his adventures: some incredible hiking, snowshoe, or mountain bike trails. It therefore didn't surprise us when he took an unpaid leave-of-absence from teaching to see if he could make a business of it. He teamed up with some investment partners and tapped into a good marketing agency. He tailored his company towards outdoor adventures focused on building character. André created packages for corporate team building, unique bachelor parties, survival-skills workshops for youth and guided kayaking and canoeing tours. When he returned for one semester to teach he said it was a slow start but he couldn't imagine doing anything else. He left teaching to continue with his business and although I can no longer find a trace of it online fifteen years later, I see that he has pivoted into the travel industry focused on elite travel experiences.

Pura Vida, See Ya! – Marisol's Story

I met Marisol in Costa Rica in 2012. She was coincidentally also a former colleague of a friend of mine who taught in a small town in Central Ontario. Her husband had worked at an auto manufacturing plant nearby. Marisol was just ten years into her teaching career when she and her husband decided on, what some may call, a dramatic life change. They sold everything in Canada and moved to Costa Rica. They loved the weather, lifestyle and saw their future blossoming in the travel industry. Her husband, Aiden, being handy in all matters of construction, decided that they could build a vacation home with an in-law suite and rent the house during high season. With the sale of their home in Canada they had enough seed money to build their home in Costa Rica. Marisol is in charge of managing the branding, promotion and rental bookings. She also started teaching online before that became the norm. She was hired by the Minnesota Department of Education that allows both public and charter schools to hire qualified teachers regardless of residency. From time to time she would have to fly to the States to participate in professional development. Just recently I checked in on how Marisol and Aiden are doing and two houses have been added to their vacation rental business. They have a steady income, especially in high season. Marisol doesn't even give it a second thought that she walked away from teaching in Canada. She and her husband are living their best life.

Downhill All the Way – Ted's Story

We know from the popular TV show Ted Lasso that "football is life". However, for this Ted, it is skiing. Today we can find Ted on the slopes in the Rocky Mountains most days. His partner shares his love for skiing and together they have become not only certified to teach skiing, they have specialized skills to work with adaptive skiers. They have also decided to convert part of their home into a bed and breakfast that will allow for passive income. This is especially ideal since they live near major ski resorts and the demand for lodging is high. So while leaving a full-time teaching position, Ted still uses all his skills working with those seeking to learn or perfect their ability to ski. Off-season, part-time work helps supplement his income but he truly feels he is able to follow his passion and live comfortably. When I asked if he is worried about aging out of the sport, he laughs and says, "My boss is twenty years older than me!"

Building A Different Portfolio – Davin's Story

I met Davin during my year of training at the Faculty of Education. He excelled in his ability to break down difficult concepts and teach someone else to grasp new knowledge and skills. He was particularly skilled in technology and became not only a lead teacher but a consultant as well. Although we did not work in the same School District we did cross paths from time to time, whether at a conference or a Ministry event. Needless to say, to my great surprise, Davin pivoted from teaching full-time into his new career path. While still working as a full-time teacher, he and his partner had started to invest in real estate property as passive income. He knew he could pivot from full-time teaching to managing his real estate portfolio, continuing to invest and teach others. He wrote a book and is a frequent guest on various podcasts providing insights to his technique of real-estate investing. I don't think there is a day that Davin regrets leaving his full-time teaching job as he still has a partial Teacher pension coming his way once he hits the right age for the more than fifteen years he worked in education.

From Classroom Teacher to Social Worker – Hailey's Story

Hailey comes from a family of educators. Stepping into the family business was a no-brainer. However, for Hailey, she discovered quite quickly that her generation of teachers were faced with many more challenges than her predecessors. Family events where the elder generation of educators confirmed that teachers are expected to wear many more 'hats' than before, had Hailey reflecting on what aspects she enjoyed most about teaching. She came to the conclusion that with her talents and skills, she'd serve children, youth, adults and families much better as a social worker than teacher. Returning to school to achieve the required credentials, Hailey pivoted into social work quite seamlessly. Although she had taught for less than ten years, she credits the ability to use that experience and skillset to transition to her new career. She has absolutely no regrets.

Whom Shall We Elect? – Reagan's Story

There are many teachers who are passionate about social justice issues and become activists or involved in their local association as a way to contribute their ideas and make positive changes. Reagan has always been a vocal advocate and decided to run for local municipal office. To Reagan's joy and somewhat surprise, they were voted in on local council.   While still working full time, they juggled attending meetings and responding to constituent outreach.   Although the School Board was somewhat accommodating in the first term, when Reagan won a second term, they decided to request an approved leave-of-absence which was granted. Now that Reagan has retired, they have their sights set on continuing to be politically involved. Serving on several non-profit boards, Reagan is also considering a run for provincial office. They continue to advocate for a strong public education system and other social justice causes. They wouldn't be the first teacher-turned-politician!

It's Wine for Me! No More Whine – Axten's Story

It's five o'clock somewhere is a great tagline if you are in the cocktail or wine business. Axten thought so too and as a high-school business teacher he had been itching to find a sustainable small business idea that he could pivot to relatively soon into his teaching career. Before having taught ten years, Axten did indeed pull the plug on teaching and start his own winemaking business.   Customers would come to his location and sign up to make their own wine. He would coach them and keep an eye on the production to ensure that customers' batches would turn out as they expected.   Axten's business was successful and was sold after about ten years when he decided he wanted to progress to helping others start their own small business. He transitioned to becoming a business coach with great success and although he has scaled back quite a bit from taking on new clients, he still provides coaching services for those who want to start a home-based or local business.

It's Changed So Much – Heather's Story

Stay in education long enough and you will notice initiatives, strategies or the theory-de-jour make a comeback. Stay long enough and you will notice that the behaviour and needs of students are increasing and the stress of having to meet all those needs is just too much. It is not difficult to understand why teachers choose to leave this stressful, work environment. Heather had been taking deferred leaves over the past ten years and really noticed how her health improved when she was removed from the school environment. Although she loves teaching, the politics, the student misbehaviour, the lack of parental support and the rotating administrators in the school created an environment that was both toxic and unhealthy for her. Heather was within a stone's throw of early retirement but the thought of returning to the classroom after her most recent deferred leave left her searching for alternatives. That is when she decided to take the cumulative value of her pension and restructure her life. Having always been a minimalist and frugal, she knew she could make her new lifestyle work for her, and most importantly her health would be prioritized. With an elderly father who requires care, he was able to move in with her and have his rent go to her instead of a stranger. Heather will continue to substitute and tutor to supplement her income. She is also a gifted musician who has had some gigs playing at special events. Although she could have 'stuck it out' until early retirement became available to her, she is happy she made the decision so that she could take back control of her life.

From the Principal's Office to HR – Kari's Story

Kari has an ambitious nature. She wanted to excel at teaching and leadership, jumping from classroom to principal in no time. By her late thirties she had already been a principal for over five years. While working full time she earned human resource credentials which eventually allowed her to pivot from education into a position for recruiting and hiring. Kari has since been gaining experience and enhancing her skills and looks forward to possibly becoming a freelancer once she retires. The world, post-pandemic, is seeing many changes to work environments and HR specialists are in demand for full-time and contract work. Kari is happy with her decision to pivot and really enjoys her work as a recruiter.

Apple On Your Desk…Top – Tasia's Story

The cliché of receiving an apple on your desk may have a different meaning these days if it was of the Macintosh computer variety. At the very beginning of Apple's campaign of integrating their products into the education system, Tasia was definitely an early adopter. By 2007 she had pivoted from teaching in one of the biggest districts in Canada to being Apple's enthusiastic liaison to School Districts and demonstrating the impact of technology in the classroom, using Apple products. Tasia had an impressive track record as a classroom teacher. Her students were always on the cutting edge of using and mastering new technology. They were one of the first groups of students to create their own movies that were posted on what was then a relatively new platform: YouTube. Tasia told me that she loved what she did because she would get to accompany senior management from school districts to exemplary schools around North America to demonstrate the impact of technology on student learning. In her role she continued to have opportunities to team-teach with teachers across Canada and was really energized by her consultant role. Needless to say, corporate life appealed to Tasia and she never looked back.

The Lessons Others' Experiences Can Teach Us

As teachers our job is to convey new concepts that hopefully resonate with our students. We do this best through storytelling or bringing things to life in a way that connects to our students' lives. Likewise, as lifelong learners ourselves, we too are eager to learn from others' experiences. What you have read in this chapter are only a handful of personal stories that I came across in my decades of teaching. If you have been contemplating and reflecting on whether to stay or go, you owe it to yourself to seriously consider the pros and cons (as discussed in Chapter 5) and explore by talking to those who have done it. When making an informed decision and taking that calculated risk, you won't regret your decision. As one of my guests on the *85 After School* podcast said "You can always go back to teaching". From what you've read though in this chapter, no one does – at least not full time.

Part 3

Appendices and Endnotes

Appendix 1 – Reading List

The following list of resources helped the author understand simple concepts of financial planning and what are typical strategies in building wealth.   The list is not exhaustive; it merely serves as a good source of Canadian-focused advice from professionals in the field of finance. You are always encouraged to seek out professional advice for your specific goals and needs.

1. Chevreau, J. (2013). MoneySense Beginner's Guide to Personal Finance.

This easy-to-read guide covers topics on: savings, debts, home and car ownership, investment steps, insurance and taxes and retirement planning.   If you are unfamiliar with the various savings methods or basic strategies of investing, this is a great start to increasing your financial literacy and vocabulary.

2. Aston, D. (2020). The Sleep-Easy Retirement Guide: Answers to the 12 Biggest Financial Questions That Keep You Up at Night.

This book covers the major financial questions in preparation for retirement. It expels suggestions and advice on how to attain enough wealth for the type of lifestyle you envision.   It also specifically discusses Canadian saving vehicles such as CPP, OAS RRSP, TFSA and more.

3. Roy, D. (2015). The essential guide to retirement readiness: Finances, Health & Wellness, Relationships, Life Purpose.

What I like about this book that differs from other financial or retirement-focused books is that it really delves into helping the reader look at their finances as part of the bigger picture. It centres on one's health, wellness, relationships, passion or life-purpose and guides the readers to reflect on their own needs and wants for retirement. From there the reader is provided with many tangible activities to guide them through the planning phases in preparation for a fulfilling retirement.

4. Sellery, B. (2014). The Moolala Guide to Rockin' Your RRSP.

Don't let the title throw you off. Similar to the book above, this book inserts reflection and tasks to organize and develop your retirement plan. We know teachers have a defined-benefit pension, which leaves us with little RRSP room. Hence, some of the strategies or suggestions may not be the best fit. It is still a worthwhile read, especially if you are growing a side hustle or small business.

5. Leung, B., & Shen, K. (2019). Quit like a millionaire: No Gimmicks, Luck, or Trust Fund Required. Hachette UK.

As part of the FIRE movement, this book provides the personal experience of two software engineers (i.e. they made way more money than teachers) who quit in their thirties. If anything, it is an entertaining read peppered with solid advice that should be in everyone's saving habits. It is chalk-full of examples and personal anecdotes from which the reader can take intended or unintended learning. One thing to remember with the FIRE (and now CoastFIRE) movement is that many of these individuals just find other sources of income: passive income from a website, selling courses, products, writing, presenting... or the like. In my opinion, they have become entrepreneurs and are not technically retired.

Appendix 2 – Basic Need Budget Template

Basic needs are often referred to as non-discretionary expenses. We all need to eat, be clothed and sheltered. When you dig a little deeper you'll recognize that there are many more subcategories in paying for a place to live, the food we eat and ensuring you have enough clothes for work and leisure. The template provides a starting point. Remember certain costs in retirement will decrease (e.g. fuel for commuting, wardrobe costs) while other categories may increase (e.g. travel, dining out, recreation) due to shift in lifestyle. This is a starting point of where you are at right now so you have a ballpark idea of how much you spend on a monthly basis to determine if your monthly pension payments will cover the basics.

Non-Discretionary Expenses: Meeting Your Obligations Before You Have Leftover to Spend As You Please

Home	Amount	Explanation
Mortgage or Rent		If you pay a biweekly mortgage, multiply by 26 then divide by 12 to get your monthly amount.
Insurance		Either home or renter's insurance. If you pay annually, just divide by 12.
Property Tax & School Tax		N/A for renters. Homeowners total the installments and divide by 12.
Water/Electricity/Gas		Add up your utility costs. Renters you may have all or some of these costs included in your rent.
Phone/Internet/ Cable/Streaming Service		
Maintenance (N/A for renters)		Add up your total costs in a year and divide by 12. Remember if you just did your roof for example, that is an anomaly that happens once every 15-20 years or so.
Car		

Loan		If you have a lease or loan that's paid bi-weekly, multiply by 26 then divide by 12.
Insurance		If you pay annually, just divide by 12.
Fuel		If you're unsure, track it for a month or multiply the average cost of a tank by the number of times you fill up in a month.
Maintenance		Track costs annually (including tire swaps etc.) and divide by 12.
Parking/Toll		Costs incurred for work purposes etc. For personal outings, do not include these costs here.
Public Transportation		If you do not own a car or combine personal vehicle and public transportation.
Groceries		
Store Bought		

Dining/Take-Out		These costs add up much more quickly than store-bought groceries to make meals at home. Hence I technically would categorize it as discretionary but many lifestyles include dining/take-out as a 'need'.
Personal Care & Clothing		
Beauty/Personal Care Items		Anything from shampoo to vitamins to haircuts.
Needed Clothing		You need new boots because your old ones have holes. (Not the tenth pair of running shoes to fill your closet).
Debt Repayment & Other		
Student Loans		
Personal Line of Credit		
Alimony/Child Support		
Total:		Once you sum your non-discretionary expenses, what is left over?

Appendix 3 – Personal Goals in Retirement

The purpose of reflecting on your personal goals for retirement beyond the financial aspect is to ensure you will have a happy, healthy, active and engaging life beyond work. This ten-minute activity will help you start identifying your personal goals. For one-on-one coaching, you can always turn to a life coach. You can also join the *85 After School* Facebook group and reach out to the author directly.

1. Which one of these activities excites you the most?

(a) becoming or maintaining my healthy fitness routine

(b) teaching others a new skill

(c) writing or creating media

(d) traveling to new places close to home or abroad

2. Complete the sentence:

Life is meaningless without ______________. (Can't think of anything? Choose one from the list).

(a) Loved ones (family, friends, kids, grandkids)

(b) Health (if I'm not healthy I can't participate meaningfully in life)

(c) Travel (I have to be able to explore the world to know myself)

(d) Activities (I need to be able to meet people, socialize, be part of something)

(e) Be Needed (I want to help others, give back, find an altruistic purpose)

(f) Creativity (I need to express myself artistically through art, photography, sewing, design, music etc.)

3. My loved ones would describe me as: __________________.
(or choose one from the list)
(a) introvert
(b) extrovert
(c) explorer
(d) problem solver
(e) helper
(f) family-oriented

4. If you won the lottery, how would you spend your time?

5. What stereotype about retirement do you want to avoid the most?
(a) boring with no stories
(b) senior centre joiner
(c) eternal traveler
(d) golfer
(e) overbearing (grand)parent

(f) couch potato TV watcher

(g) fatigued

(h) lonely

(i) none

6.   If you were granted one wish, what would it be?

7.   What do you miss most about your younger years?
(a) accomplishments at work
(b) motivation level & energy
(c) active calendar of events
(d) clarity and structure of long term goals
(e) being strong and healthier
(f) interaction with lots of people

8.   How concerned are you about making goals that will take you into retirement?
(a) I'm doing this reflection for fun
(b) I'm doing this reflection because I need some guidance
(c) I'm doing this reflection because I really want to set goals for retirement

9.   In #4 you indicated how you would spend your time if you won the lottery. One of the things you listed as an activity is:

_________________________.

What do you need (i.e. skills, materials or other) in order to achieve that goal?

Skills	Materials / Tangibles	Other

10. Write a SMART goal to commit towards achieving the goal. An example is:

One of the activities I listed is becoming a more advanced yoga practitioner.

Skills	Materials / Tangibles	Other
- Become more familiar with yoga techniques - Developing a stronger core	- better equipment (e.g. mat and yoga blocks)	- Commitment to practise at least four times a week - Find a good instructor

Specific
Measurable
Attainable
Realistic
Timely

Within one year of retiring, I will be an intermediate yoga practitioner, being able to hold at least five of the most difficult poses double the amount of time than now, by practising four times a week with Stacy, my instructor.

Now repeat this for other passions identified in your reflection. What jumps out that you want to do, be or learn? Hold yourself accountable but if the goal is not resonating or of interest anymore, give yourself permission to move on to an endeavour that is more your passion.

Go back to your answers for the questions in 30 days and see if anything has changed. If you notice something really does not change, that is a good indication that it is something you really wish to focus on once retired.

You can do this exercise with the intensity you desire. If you don't want to write SMART goals, don't. The point is to explore and determine what will get you excited once you can set your own schedule. You can do this on your own, in a small trusted group or reach out to a retired teacher.

Endnotes

[1] In Ontario for example, the Ontario College of Teachers has traditionally conducted an annual survey of new grads from Faculties and identified the rate of success of securing full-time employment, which subjects are in demand and, the levels of underemployment and unemployment.

[2] Surplus denotes that there is a job in the Board for you but not at your current school. Recall denotes that you do not have a job but a right to be called back to a job before a brand new hire. Redundancy denotes there is no job for you. The definitions of these words may differ in varying jurisdictions but the general use of them is to categorize a current employee or soon-to-be non-employee.

[3] Author's personal pensions statements issued in 2008 and 2013.

[4] Statistics Canada reports 4.5 million Canadians were active defined-benefit pension plan members and CEIC reports there were 19.5 million employed Canadians in 2021. This results in approximately 23% of the population having a defined-benefit pension through their employer (https://www150.statcan.gc.ca/n1/

daily-quotidien/230623/t001b-eng.htm and https://www.ceicdata.com/). Retrieved 24 March 2024.

[5] Read about the governing structure on the Ontario Teachers' Pension Plan website https://www.otpp.com/en-ca/about-us/our-plan/our-board/. Retrieved on 29 March 2024.

[6] Read more about the structure at Ontario Teachers' Federation https://www.otffeo.on.ca/en/pensions/faqs/. Retrieved 29 March 2024.

[7] Read more about Retrait Quebec https://www-retraitequebec-gouv-qc-ca.translate.goog/fr/publications/rrsp/rregop/Pages/rregop.aspx_x_tr_sl=fr&_x_tr_tl=en&_x_tr_hl=en&_x_tr_pto=sc. Retrieved 7 Jan 2024.

[8] Visit https://www.atrf.com/ and specifically the videos for beginning teachers https://vimeo.com/showcase/10671612 Retrieved 9 Jan 2024.

[9] Average salary was retrieved from https://www150.statcan.gc.ca/t1/tbl1/en/tv.action?pid=3710024301 on 9 Jan 2024 Annual statutory teachers' salaries in public institutions

[10] Although this research had respondents from the United States only, the principle can be applied to Canadian teachers. Read the article here: https://moneywise.com/employment/employment/you-cant-outearn-stupidity-hybrid?

utm_source=syn_applenews_mon&utm_medium=Z&utm_campaign=5
4072&utm_content=syn_b0921ce9-628b-4a9e-a777-b048010672af.
Retrieved on 27 May 2024.

[11] $1,500 invested at a rate of 4% over 25 years with an estimated 2.9% inflation rate would provide me simple interest of $1,500 (doubling my money) and compounded interest of $999 bringing my total investment to $3,999 (calculated using https://www.bankrate.com/retirement/roi-calculator/). Retrieved on 9 Jan 2024.

[12] There are many self-administered tests online that you can take to determine your leadership style. These provide insight but you know yourself best. Being honest about your strengths and weaknesses allow you to focus on learning and growing in the areas that need enhancement. Try the University of Massachusetts Global quiz as a starting point to help understand your leadership style (https://www.umassglobal.edu/news-and-events/blog/what-type-of-leader-are-you-quiz). Retrieved on 29 March 2024.

[13] I am not a financial advisor or by any means a professional from whom you should take financial advice. I am speaking from personal experience and giving a personal opinion.   You should always consult with a professional to determine what is the best for you given your unique situation. To clarify, I am suggesting a couple to save 15%-20% of their net income and singles to save 10%-15% of their net income if they can afford it.

[14] You can join our online community and learn how to put a financial and personal portfolio together focused on a five and ten year plan. Reach out to the author on Facebook or Instagram.

[15] I have used the basic calculator from the Sun Life website but any similar calculator will do the trick. (https://www.sunlife.ca/en/tools-and-resources/tools-and-calculators/net-worth-calculator/) Retrieved 29 March 2024.

[16] You can also join our online community and learn how to put a financial and personal portfolio together focused on a five and ten year plan. Reach out to the author on Facebook or Instagram.

[17] The OTTP's 2023 Annual Report, p. 56 https://www.otpp.com/content/dam/otpp/documents/reports/2023-ar/otpp-2023-annual-report-eng.pdf. Retrieved on 29 March 2024.

[18] Selection of careers listed on Indeed retrieved on 1 March 2024 https://ca.indeed.com/career-advice/finding-a-job/alternative-careers-for-teachers

[19] Adapted from 7 Quick Tips to Make the Transition retrieved from https://www.uopeople.edu/blog/10-alternative-careers-for-teachers/

[20] If you would like to have a simplified list, the Government of Manitoba provides it at: https://www.edu.gov.mb.ca/k12/profcert/province.html Retrieved 29 March 2024.

About the Author

Nicole van Woudenberg is an award-winning teacher with over 25 years experience in education. Licensed in several jurisdictions, Nicole has worked at the elementary and high school levels in Ontario and Québec. She has held various leadership positions, including consultant, vice-principal and as Chair at the Ontario College of Teachers.

Nicole has served as a board member for several non-profit boards. Her knowledge in policy development and serving on various committees including finance, accreditation, legislation and quality assurance have contributed to positive changes and practices.

Over the span of her career she has authored, edited and published teacher guides, policy and procedure manuals, a newsletter serial as well as produced multi-faceted instructional videos for teacher-learning.

Her current project, the *85 After School* podcast, features retired teachers sharing their insights and passions post-teaching. Nicole continues to develop resources for educational practitioners which you can find through the *85 After School* media profiles.